W9-AUU-105

No More Culturally
Irrelevant Teaching

Dear Readers,

Much like the diet phenomenon *Eat This, Not That*, this series aims to replace some existing practices with approaches that are more effective—healthier, if you will—for our students. We hope to draw attention to practices that have little support in research or professional wisdom and offer alternatives that have greater support. Each text is collaboratively written by authors representing research and practice. Section 1 offers practitioners' perspectives on a practice in need of replacing and helps us understand the challenges, temptations, and misunderstandings that have led us to this ineffective approach. Section 2 provides a researcher's perspective on the lack of research to support the ineffective practice(s) and reviews research supporting better approaches. In Section 3, the authors representing practitioners' perspectives give detailed descriptions of how to implement these better practices. By the end of each book, you will understand both what not to do, and what to do, to improve student learning.

It takes courage to question one's own practice—to shift away from what you may have seen throughout your years in education and toward something new that you may have seen few if any colleagues use. We applaud you for demonstrating that courage and wish you the very best in your journey from this to that.

Best wishes,

—Ellin Oliver Keene and Nell K. Duke, series editors

No More Culturally Irrelevant Teaching

MARIANA SOUTO-MANNING

CARMEN LUGO LLERENA

JESSICA MARTELL

ABIGAIL SALAS MAGUIRE

ALICIA ARCE-BOARDMAN

HEINEMANN
Portsmouth, NH

Heinemann
361 Hanover Street
Portsmouth, NH 03801–3912
www.heinemann.com

Offices and agents throughout the world

© 2018 by Mariana Souto-Manning, Alicia Boardman, Carmen Llerena, Jessica Martell, and Abigail Salas

All rights reserved. No part of this book may be reproduced in any form or by any electronic or mechanical means, including information storage and retrieval systems, without permission in writing from the publisher, except by a reviewer, who may quote brief passages in a review.

> *The authors have dedicated a great deal of time and effort to writing the content of this book, and their written expression is protected by copyright law. We respectfully ask that you do not adapt, reuse, or copy anything on third-party (whether for-profit or not-for-profit) lesson-sharing websites.*
> *As always, we're happy to answer any questions you may have.*
> **—Heinemann Publishers**

"Dedicated to Teachers" is a trademark of Greenwood Publishing Group, Inc.

Library of Congress Cataloging-in-Publication Data
Names: Souto-Manning, Mariana, author.
  Title: No more culturally irrelevant teaching / Mariana Souto-Manning, Carmen
  Lugo Llerena, Jessica Martell, Abigail Salas Maguire, Alicia Arce-Boardman.
Description: Portsmouth, NH : Heinemann, 2018. | Series: Not this but that |
  Includes bibliographical references.
Identifiers: LCCN 2017043353 | ISBN 9780325089799
  Subjects: LCSH: Culturally relevant pedagogy—United States. | Education,
  Elementary—Social aspects—United States.
Classification: LCC LC1099.3 .S637 2018 | DDC 370.117—dc23

LC record available at https://lccn.loc.gov/2017043353

Series Editors: Ellin Oliver Keene *and* Nell K. Duke
Acquisitions Editor: Katie Wood Ray
Production Editor: Sean Moreau
Cover Design: Lisa Fowler
Cover Images: boy (both poses): michael jung—stock.adobe.com; *classroom*: Tyler Olson—stock.adobe.com; *mirror*: msharova—stock.adobe.com
Interior Design: Suzanne Heiser
Typesetter: Valerie Levy, Drawing Board Studios
Manufacturing: Val Cooper

Printed in the United States of America on acid-free paper
22 21 20 19 18 VP 1 2 3 4 5

CONTENTS

Introduction Ellin Oliver Keene   viii

SECTION 1   **NOT THIS**

1

When Culture Comes to School
Carmen Lugo Llerena, Jessica Martell,
Abigail Salas Maguire, and Alicia Arce-Boardman

Scene from a Classroom: An Anthology About White Royalty in an
Urban Kindergarten   2

- *What's the Problem?*   4

Scene from a Classroom: Picture Books That Lack Cultural Authenticity   6

- *What's the Problem?*   7

The Importance of Windows *and* Mirrors   8

Why Does Culturally Irrelevant Teaching Persist?   9

- *The Expectations of Mandated, Standardized Curriculum*   10

- *The Pressure of High-Stakes Testing*   10

- *The Access to Materials: Our Demographic Reality Versus Our Curriculum*   11

- *A Lack of Cultural Understanding*   12

- *A Fear of Engaging in Culturally Relevant Teaching*   12

- *The Issue of Time*   13

It Doesn't Have to Be This Way   14

SECTION 2   **WHY NOT? WHAT WORKS?**

16

**Understanding the Power, Possibility, and
Effectiveness of Culturally Relevant and
Responsive Teaching**
Mariana Souto-Manning

The Mismatch of Culture and Curriculum   17

Ignoring Culture in the Classroom Disadvantages Students   20

Mindset Shifts: Undoing Cultural Assumptions That Impact Teaching and Learning   24

- *Move Away from "Saving Students"*   24

- *Challenge the Idea of a Race- or Culture-Based Achievement Gap*   25

- *Rewrite the Metaphor for Achievement: It's a Debt, Not a Gap!*   27

- *Reposition Culture as Additive, Not Subtractive*   27

Defining Culturally Relevant and Responsive Teaching   28

- *Culturally Responsive Teaching: A Focus on Teacher Practice*   29

- *Culturally Relevant Pedagogy: A Focus on Teacher Mindset and Cultural Understanding*   30

Make the Move to Culturally Relevant Teaching   31

- *Student Learning*   31

- *Cultural Competence*   38

- *Critical Consciousness*   43

The Effectiveness of Culturally Relevant Teaching Across Content Areas   46

Engaging in Culturally Relevant Teaching   46

Section 3   **BUT THAT**

Strategies, Tools, and Practices for Culturally Relevant Teaching

52

Carmen Lugo Llerena, Jessica Martell, Abigail Salas Maguire, and Alicia Arce-Boardman

A Mindset for Culturally Relevant Teaching   53

What's in a Name?   54

- *First Things First: Learn to Pronounce Students' Names*   54

- *Tap into Family Literacies: An Inquiry into the History of Names*   56

Rethinking Hispanic Heritage Month   60

- *Artifactual Literacy: Every Object Has a Story*   61

- *Video: A Power Tool for Developing Cross-Cultural Understandings*   63

Learning from Classroom Interviews   65

- *Funds of Knowledge: Who Do We Have Here?*   65

- *Teaching Students to Interview*   67

Elevating the *Story* in His*tory*   70

- *Read-Aloud as a Tool to Trouble the Single Story*   71
- *Experiencing Multiple Perspectives Through Story Acting*   73

Culturally Relevant Teaching Is Essential, Now More Than Ever   76

Afterword Nell K. Duke   78

References   80

INTRODUCTION

Ellin Oliver Keene

During a recent visit to a city where I was working in schools, I decided to do what I often do when traveling—hunt down an independent children's bookstore. I travel with a suitcase roughly twice the size of what I need and often head home with some gems—recent and vintage titles—to share with students on my next trip. I wonder if one can write off the luggage overweight charges on one's taxes?! Something to think about....

In this city, I found a children's bookshop and headed that direction after school. I noticed the "multicultural" section and began to browse. Sure enough, the titles reflected the issues you're about to read in Section 1. There were books depicting holidays and festivals from several cultures; a book of dolls in "traditional dress" from a variety of countries (mostly European); there were books written by white authors *about* people of color, but only three—three—titles that meet the standards the authors of this book set for materials that are culturally relevant. I mentioned this issue to the proprietor who seemed to misunderstand. She redirected me to the "multicultural" section and asked if she could help.

She *can* help, as we all can. Carmen, Jessica, Abigail, and Alicia, coauthors of Sections 1 and 3 in this book, suggest that, to engage in culturally relevant teaching, we must first consider our *mindset* toward children. It comes down to what we believe, in our heart of hearts, about every child's capacity to think at high levels and engage deeply in learning.

These authors walk their talk. In every word of this book, all five authors consistently use asset-based language, and it made me realize how many times a *day* we use or hear deficit language about children. I urge you to keep track of deficit language—just for a day or two. You'll be shocked.

The authors' mindset of unencumbered belief in children shines through these pages and makes the reader aware of the subtle cultural biases present in so many classrooms. Their examples made me wince, knowing that I have perpetuated culturally *irrelevant* teaching at different moments in my career, and they caused me to rethink the work I do when I am in classrooms now, no matter the cultural and racial makeup of the school.

In Section 2, Mariana points out that there is no such thing as *acultural* teaching. Every move we make in the classroom has cultural implications, and culturally relevant teaching practices make a difference for students—the research on this is clear. We know, for example, that children's engagement and reading performance improve when they read books and engage in a range of classroom and community practices in which their stories are told and honored (Au 1980). Souto-Manning provides dozens of other studies that support culturally relevant teaching.

Mariana's review of the research caused me to wonder why anyone would avoid culturally relevant teaching. In one especially potent paragraph, she describes a study (Bishop 1990) in which the author:

> explains that children must see themselves in classroom texts so they can affirm their identities and practices and feel that they belong. Reading can become "a means of self-affirmation" if readers find "mirrors in books" (ix), yet, Bishop reminds us that in 1990, "6,340,000 nonwhite children are learning to read and to understand the American way of life in books which either omit them entirely or scarcely mention them." (ix)

Is it any better now? Over 50 percent of students in American schools are students of color.

Has the move toward culturally relevant teaching reached all of them? Even if Bishop's statistics have improved, we can still assume that we have a long way to go after reading Section 1. It is simply vital that children tell stories, see visuals and artifacts, and, importantly, read and listen to books that represent them and are authored by people who look like them.

Having a handful of "multicultural" picture books is not enough, however, as I hope the aforementioned bookshop owner has discovered. Carmen, Jessica, Abigail, and Alicia explore some wholly original and fascinating approaches that go beyond read-alouds.

Wait until you get to the section about children bringing their "artifactual histories" into the classroom or the section in which "story acting" is used to help children understand oppression! The authors underscore the importance of narrative; we need to bring the stories of children's lives outside the classroom into our everyday work with children. They go on to address the need for counternarratives. Whose voices provide a different perspective than those we're accustomed to hearing? Whose voices are missing completely? I was captivated by the students' work shared in Section 3 and know you'll be able to extrapolate from these approaches to your classroom.

This is a book about disrupting perceptions and preconceived notions about children and teaching practice. It's the kind of book I treasure and reread precisely because it is disruptive. In this, one of the most deliciously diverse countries in the world, there is an urgency to move toward culturally relevant teaching. This book will light the path of your journey.

SECTION 1

NOT THIS

When Culture Comes to School

CARMEN LUGO LLERENA, JESSICA MARTELL, ABIGAIL SALAS MAGUIRE, AND ALICIA ARCE-BOARDMAN

Alicia was a child whose parents immigrated to the United States from Paraguay and Mexico. As she grew up and attended a public elementary school, Alicia was not exposed to culturally relevant teaching. She only remembers hearing about Cinco de Mayo as a student, a day that was not meaningful to her or her family. Regardless, her peers and teachers *thought* that Cinco de Mayo was an important holiday for her, communicating to her their lack of knowledge about the diversities within and across Latinx communities. Hispanic Heritage Month was never really recognized or celebrated during her

> *Latinx* is a gender-inclusive term referring to people with cultural ties to Latin America and of Latin American descent. The term *Hispanic* refers to people from Spanish-speaking countries; it is seen as problematic by many (due to its references to colonization).

schooling either—not even in shallow or marginal ways. As a result, Alicia felt invisible. She felt that her history, home language, and family culture did not matter.

Alicia grew up to become a public school teacher, as each of us did—Carmen, Jessica, and Abigail—committed to making Latinx students' histories and identities integral in both our classrooms and the life of our schools. We share this commitment with lots of other teachers, we know, but it's also important to recognize that many preschools and schools *do not* acknowledge students' cultures in any distinct way. Others engage in this important work along a continuum, from those who introduce cultural diversity in one-time events at specific times, such as the designated Hispanic Heritage Month or Black History Month, to those who've changed their curriculum to focus on cultural and racial justice, embracing equity at the center of teaching—and everything in between.

What is your school like? Chances are, if you're reading this book, your school may need to begin considering culturally relevant teaching, may have begun thinking about it, or may be enacting culturally relevant teaching at specific times. Regardless of your starting point, the first step to making a change is understanding what needs to change—and why. Let's start our exploration of that question with stories from kindergarten and second grade that illustrate how well-meaning teachers may unintentionally fail to recognize their students as cultural beings.

Scene from a Classroom: An Anthology About White Royalty in an Urban Kindergarten

With her kindergarten students gathered in front of her, Ms. Smith began, "Friends, today we start a new read-aloud. We will be learning about kings and queens." In a Title I New York City public school, Ms. Smith's students were mostly African American and Latinx. The children sat crisscross applesauce on the rug as they were told about their new unit of study. For the next few weeks they would listen to read-alouds about kings and queens. Almost immediately the children reacted to the news with mixed reactions—squeals of enthusiasm, groans in protest, and silent indifference.

The initial excitement of some children was quickly tarnished when one student's spontaneous comment disrupted Ms. Smith's introduction. The student pointed to the illustration in the reading anthology where she'd noticed that the characters portrayed were all White. She immediately declared, "We gonna learn about princesses like Tiffany," identifying the only White girl in the classroom.

"Uh-uh," another child loudly called out while crossing her arms and shaking her head. "I can be a princess too," she said, swaying her long box braids from side to side.

"You wish! You're not like a princess, you know," Shenetta declared.

This quick introduction to a new read-aloud unit that aligned with the mandated curriculum had made visible who is often present and who is invisible in read-alouds and in curriculum at large. For the next few weeks, Ms. Smith's kindergartners were expected to learn about the responsibilities of a royal family, the advantages and disadvantages of children born into royal families, the royal objects they possessed, and where they lived long ago.

Regaining the attention of her class, Ms. Smith began the lesson by showing the children where Europe is on a world map. They were told they would be listening to a read-aloud about several kings and queens who lived in Europe many years ago. When Ms. Smith began the read-aloud, her students, who ranged in age from four to six years old, were expected to sit quietly and listen. During the reading, the students were shown images of a palace, King Richard II, a crown, and Charlemagne, and they were exposed to new vocabulary words—*servant* and *royal*. The children were not discouraged from asking questions during the reading, but they were not asked to share their thoughts or connections with the class or their "turn and talk" partners. After the reading, the teacher asked multiple literal and inferential questions.

By the end of the lesson, the students seemed interested in just about anything *but* the read-aloud. They had been sitting on the rug for over twenty minutes, and they were candid with their feedback. One said, "That was boring!" Another declared, "That was too long!" It was no surprise that many were not able to answer the comprehension questions that followed the reading. In fact, shortly after the read-aloud began, few children were actively listening, despite Ms. Smith reminding them often to have whole body listening while she was reading.

The students' lack of interest in the read-aloud stood in stark contrast to how they listened to books such as Duncan Tonatiuh's *The Princess and the Warrior: A Tale of Two Volcanoes*. With both informational texts and stories, the children were partial to picture books that contained ideas, characters, and themes they could relate to, and the opening read-aloud for their kings and queens unit just hadn't resonated with them. Could something else have connected them more to the reading? Maybe, but there were no discussions about the author and illustrator, no predictions made, no previewing the pictures, and no turn and talks during the actual reading. Students who had breaks built into their schedules (as outlined in their IEPs, or individualized education programs) were quick to remind Ms. Smith that it was time for a break, and children who didn't usually ask for breaks did too. There were certainly no requests for the text to be read again or for it to be added to the classroom library.

What's the Problem?

Imagine that practically every day you go to school, you are asked to read or listen to something that is not representative of who you are, of your family, or of your community. The books put in front of you just don't reflect your interests or your life in any way. Imagine being told to remain silent as these books are shared. For twice as many minutes as your age! Sound absurd? What would you do? Tune out? Daydream? Take a break? Talk with a peer? Misbehave? Does it make you wonder how children feel in a similar situation? This was Ms. Smith's kindergartners' daily classroom experience, and sadly, this is very common in kindergarten classes.

The curriculum was comprised of many units that did not appeal to—or even consider—the children sitting in front of the teacher. The stories did not portray diverse ways of being and behaving. They did not have diverse characters. Issues immediately relevant to the children Ms. Smith taught were absent—as were their images, cultural practices, histories, and communities.

The unit on kings and queens was closely aligned with mandated standards, but the focus on coverage rather than mastery of skills meant that although Ms. Smith covered the standards, the children didn't necessarily develop skills because they had no investment in the content. Instead of learning about who they are—their heritages and histories—the children in Ms. Smith's kindergarten classroom were learning other people's histories. They did not see themselves reflected in the stories and quickly lost interest.

Ms. Smith was using the reading anthology provided to support the mandated standards, but in fact, almost nothing in the list of skills students were supposed to develop in the unit was tied directly to the particular stories in the anthology (reciting "Old King Cole" and "Sing a Song of Sixpence" are the notable exceptions). For example, by the end of the unit, students were supposed to:

> **Research shows both the underrepresentation and misrepresentation of minoritized populations in reviews of textbooks.**
>
> See Section 2, page 18.

Describe what a king or queen does.
Identify and describe royal objects associated
    with a king or queen.
Describe a royal family.

Nothing in this list suggests a focus on the kings and queens from Europe (those included in the anthology). Stories or informational texts about royal families the world over and throughout history—like the beloved picture book *The Princess and the Warrior*—might just as well help children develop these understandings. In fact, only the first ten skills in the mandated curriculum have anything to do with kings and queens at all! The other thirty-eight are more general reading skills such as "Describe the characters, settings, and plots in fiction read-alouds" and "Actively engage in fiction read-alouds."

Actively engage in fiction read-alouds. The problem is, as long as all the teaching comes from materials that were selected and developed far away from the students who use them, active engagement is likely to be a challenge. It would be nice if the solution were as simple as swapping anthologies for high-interest picture books, but it's actually more complicated than that. Sometimes even when teachers do select their own materials with their students' cultural practices in mind, problems arise, as you'll see in the next scene from a classroom.

Scene from a Classroom: Picture Books That Lack Cultural Authenticity

Ms. Garza teaches in a suburb of New York City in a school serving a predominantly White middle- and upper-income community, which has recently experienced a surge in Latinx immigrant families. As she gathered her twenty-three dual language second graders on her classroom rug to introduce an author study of Ann Whitford Paul, she opened the book, *Mañana Iguana*, an English text with Spanish words inserted throughout. When the children were ready, she began reading, "'On martes,' Iguana asked, 'Who will help me deliver the invitations for our *fiesta*?'"

After reading *Mañana Iguana,* Ms. Garza demonstrated how she planned for writing her own narrative featuring a Mexican iguana. She anticipated her students would make personal connections between their own experiences with Latinx culture and the characters portrayed by author Ann Whitford Paul. Her goal was to have students develop ideas and eventually produce a narrative featuring Latinx characters for Hispanic Heritage Month.

As she sent her students to write independently, Ms. Garza pointed to a basket labeled "Hispanic Heritage," and she said, "You may choose any book from this basket." The basket contained copies of *Mañana Iguana, Count on Culebra, Tortuga in Trouble,* and *Fiesta Fiasco,* all written by Ann Whitford Paul. As the children in the class proceeded to their tables and started to work, Ms. Garza noticed that Ana, Luis, and Yesenia lagged behind. Ana remained on the rug long after her peers moved on, seemingly sad. Her family is Mexican, but she did not seem interested in Paul's books. Yesenia, another child whose family recently emigrated from the state of Guerrero, Mexico, wandered across the classroom, touching a number of objects, but avoiding the "Hispanic Heritage" book basket. Luis, also from Mexico, opened his writing journal and doodled on a page. They were not engaged. They did not see themselves in the book Ms. Garza read.

Irma, a Latinx child whose family emigrated from Chile, turned to her friend, also Latinx, and shared, "Voy a escribir sobre los mexicanos, que son ignorantes y perezosos" [I'm going to write about the Mexicans, who are ignorant and lazy]. Her friend, whose family is Puerto Rican, giggled. Irma voiced the message presented in the book about Mexicans; a problematic single story (Adichie 2009), which perpetuates stereotypes.

What's the Problem?

Someone entering Ms. Garza's second-grade classroom may have believed her class was engaged in culturally relevant teaching and learning. They may have perceived her choice of *Mañana Iguana,* a story in which Spanish words are interspersed with English words, as an effort to validate both English and Spanish. However, the book is problematic in several ways. *Mañana Iguana* tells the traditional story of the Little Red Hen, but the characters are desert animals with Spanish names such as Iguana, Tortuga, and Culebra. Despite the effort to include Mexican characters and demonstrate cultural inclusivity, the book is not an authentic representation of Mexican people or their culture. The book not only portrays Mexicans as lazy desert animals, but the Spanish words interjected throughout (to make it seem more "Mexican") can be perceived as mocking. When we think of an inclusive and culturally relevant curriculum, we think of children being represented in accurate and genuine ways. In her well-intentioned, yet misguided, attempt to engage in culturally relevant teaching practices, the books Ms. Garza selected perpetuated stereotypes. In addition, they led children to conflate Latinx with Mexicans.

The Importance of Windows and Mirrors

The children in Ms. Smith's and Ms. Garza's classrooms could not see themselves, their communities, or their cultural practices in the stories being read. Classroom libraries and resources should honor and reflect students' diversity rather than perpetuate the stereotypes that marginalize them. Rudine Sims Bishop (1990) proposes that books and other classroom materials serve both as mirrors, reflecting one's own world, and windows, providing entryways into the world of others. Yet, when all stories and illustrations are windows, as they were in Ms. Smith's class, children do not see that they or their stories belong in the classroom and school.

> **"Ignoring Culture in the Classroom Disadvantages Students"** contains more information about the socioemotional and academic implications of culturally irrelevant teaching.
>
> See Section 2, page 20.

When there are no mirrors and everything is a window, there can be socioemotional and academic implications. Children may perceive one culture as more worthy and believe that those not represented are not valued. They may fail to engage with the curriculum at all. On the other hand, when everything is a mirror and children always see themselves in the stories they read and hear, they may develop an exaggerated sense of themselves and of their place in the world (Bishop 2015) and fail to develop empathy and understanding for different perspectives.

Children are cultural beings with amazing histories and practices, and no two children are the same. Of course, no two classes are the same either, no two schools, no two teachers. But efforts to "normalize" curriculum and "standardize" learning would seem to suggest the opposite. These efforts presume that the knowledge that counts is in the textbooks and other curricular materials. Too often these efforts leave little room for curriculum to be enhanced by the knowledge, experiences, and questions that students bring to the classroom. Too often, the standardization of schooling leaves some children perpetually peering out of windows and others gazing into mirrors.

> **Curriculum and teaching are always cultural, but they are not always culturally relevant or responsive.**

Why Does Culturally Irrelevant Teaching Persist?

The snapshots from these two classrooms address the problem of materials; but making our teaching relevant to students involves so much more than *just* materials. As you'll see in Sections 2 and 3, culturally relevant teaching is a complex web of mindsets, plans, and practices that place students at the center of all decision making. At its core, it's teaching that:

- holds high expectations
- supports learning with relevancy
- develops cultural competence
- encourages the critical questioning of injustices.

Few would argue against these important principles, but teachers still have lots of reasons for not engaging in culturally relevant teaching. We know. We've been there. "I don't have time" and "It's not gonna be on the test" have been excuses for us too. But as our schools become increasingly diverse, it's worth questioning what gets in the way of teachers planning for teaching that is relevant and responsive to the students they have in their classrooms.

The Expectations of Mandated, Standardized Curriculum

Over the course of our many years teaching, we've all experienced waves, at times full cycles, of curricula coming through our schools like revolving doors—constantly in motion. One year, we learn a new math curriculum. The next year, we implement a new reading curriculum. The year after, we start a new science curriculum. The following year, we invest in a new social studies curriculum. And, before you know it, we're throwing out the "new" math teacher's editions and opening shiny and colorful boxes of another company's recently developed units.

From *No Child Left Behind* to *Every Student Succeeds Act*. From state-based standards to the Common Core State Standards. With each new initiative, new curriculum and assessments are rolled out by publishing companies, marketed as the silver bullet for addressing the new standards, sold to schools, and expected to be implemented in classrooms. Training sessions are scheduled where "experts" who don't know our practices, our students, or our communities walk into our professional homes and attempt to sell us on a one-size-fits-all approach. Sound familiar?

Like you, we open those boxes and realize they do not include the children we teach—children with disabilities, emergent bilinguals (English language learners), children of color—but what do we do? We believe curriculum should be meaningful, engaging, relevant, and relatable to our students. We want all children to be engaged and to learn. But unfortunately, like you, the expectation that we must stick to the assigned curriculum looms large and often feels insurmountable. Against our better judgment, we find ourselves navigating mandated curriculum that is not relevant to the children we teach, failing to engage our students and wasting valuable teaching time.

The Pressure of High-Stakes Testing

The pressure to do well on standardized tests is another obstacle that can get in the way of culturally relevant teaching. In some schools, teachers are constrained by strict testing mandates, and feel obligated to follow pacing charts and assessment calendars that leave little room for student-centered engagement.

For those who teach in the grades where students are tested, the pressure can be intense, and using test prep materials may seem like the responsible thing to do. After all, with these materials everything is carefully planned out and beautifully bound in a test prep book, and students generally work quietly and independently to complete the exercises. Even when the content seems very far removed from the students using these materials—writing about the first flight across the Atlantic, for example, or stories narrated by children prancing around in a meadow—it's easy to think, "Well this is what the test is going to be like." Teachers experience a very real tension between getting students ready to take a high-stakes test—which may or may not use culturally relevant material—and preparing them to think critically and engage in meaningful and culturally relevant learning.

The Access to Materials: Our Demographic Reality Versus Our Curriculum

We all have had trouble finding good books and authentic resources. At first, we thought it was because we didn't have the knowledge. But then we realized that wasn't it. It's a far- and wide-reaching problem. Although the number of students of color in the United States has surpassed the number of White students, publishing companies continue to publish curricula that normalize the White experience. Curriculum guides and materials feature very few children of color, children with disabilities, and children from low- or no-income backgrounds.

The problem of access to culturally relevant materials is also acute in the world of trade books. Not accounting for problematic accounts and stories, in 2015 the Cooperative Children's Book Center documented that over 70 percent of children's books published were about White children and families. Sadly, only 7.6 percent were about African Americans, 3.3 percent were about Asians and Asian Americans, 2.4

percent were about Latinx, and 0.9 percent were about indigenous/ First Nations people. The remaining 12 percent of books written for children focused on something other than people—such as trucks and animals—roughly the same amount as those portraying people of color. To top it all off, not only are books about people of color harder to find, they're also more expensive. So although it would be easy to disapprove of Ms. Garza's book selection, we recognize that materials can be hard to find and many of them actually foster negative stereotypes.

A Lack of Cultural Understanding

Sometimes a lack of knowledge about other cultures is what gets in the way of culturally relevant teaching. As a construct, culture is complex and, like language, it varies from state to state, city to city, neighborhood to neighborhood, family to family, and individual to individual. Teachers like Ms. Garza may have good intentions in celebrating the diversity of culture in the classroom, but what they think qualifies as culturally relevant may in fact be perpetuating certain stereotypes. For example, a popular way teachers attempt to celebrate their students' culture is with a potluck. In this activity, families bring a dish that celebrates their culture to share with the class or school. Students may decorate the classroom or school with flags and may even dress in "traditional" clothing (or what some call "costumes"). But, how can one dish represent a whole culture? Although well-intentioned, these practices may serve to perpetuate stereotypes.

Realizing how much or how little you know about your students' cultures can be a first step toward culturally relevant teaching, but it can also lead to other obstacles, as you'll see next.

A Fear of Engaging in Culturally Relevant Teaching

As teachers, we may be reluctant to engage in culturally relevant practices because we realize we don't know enough about our students' cultures to address them meaningfully. We care about our students and we fear perpetuating stereotypes. We fear doing or saying the wrong thing. The answer to this fear, however, is simple. Becoming "culturally competent" takes time and requires us to position ourselves as learners. We don't have to know everything about every group of people to engage in this work, but we do need to be willing to learn and ready to facilitate learning about cultures in our classrooms.

> Cultural competence begins with understanding yourself as a cultural being. The questions on page 40 in Section 2 will help you get started.

Of course, we may also fear that our students aren't old enough or mature enough to understand or discuss the problems connected to culture in our society. We may fear upsetting parents when we engage their children in discussing issues of race or sexual orientation. We may fear that we will be seen as promoting our personal agendas. We may also fear that our *students* will feel uncomfortable addressing these matters, whether they directly affect the communities they live in or not. Any one of these fears can get in the way of culturally relevant teaching, so it's important to acknowledge them.

The Issue of Time

There is only so much time. As teachers, we've all had days that are a blur. The bell rings, you meet with your guided reading groups, you provide feedback on classwork, you make copies, and before you know it, it's dismissal time. You ask yourself, "Where does the day go?" and you hear your stomach rumble. Of course! You forgot to have lunch! While your students were having lunch and recess, you were busy checking homework. We get it. It happens all the time.

For most teachers, one of the main reasons culturally irrelevant teaching persists is a lack of time to prepare. We all struggle with finding time to plan meaningful and engaging lessons that represent our classroom communities. As we pointed out earlier, Ms. Smith could have easily used different resources to teach her students about kings and queens and still meet all of the objectives of the required unit. But it takes time to find those resources, time to decide how to use them, what questions to ask, what activities to plan. When we're handed an anthology with all that work already done for us, it's hard to put it aside and replace it with something we've developed with our students in mind. After all, replacing it means developing new learning experiences with new materials, and there's only so much time.

In Section 3, you'll learn lots of ways to incorporate culturally relevant practices into your existing curriculum.

Related to the issue of time is the belief that culturally relevant teaching is *one more thing to do* in an already packed schedule. We already have so much to do with the curriculum we are given; there just isn't time to add something more. For it to make sense, we have to see culturally relevant teaching as a reframing or as an overlay—not an addition—to the existing curriculum. We must think of the mandated curriculum as a starting place, not an ending place, and find ways to include new perspectives and materials, making curriculum and teaching more inclusive and representative.

It Doesn't Have to Be This Way

We have learned from our own experiences with culturally relevant teaching that although these obstacles are real, they are not impossible to overcome. As a matter of fact, once we began shifting our practices, co-planning with colleagues, and reflecting on what was and wasn't working, we found so many simple paths to this way of teaching in our day-to-day work. We also learned that students are always ready for culturally relevant teaching—they're just waiting for their teachers to be ready. Students embrace the dialogue about culture in the classroom, and they are anxiously waiting for teachers to invite them to add their voices, expeirences, and practices to curriculum and teaching.

In Section 3, we'll show you how we have brought culturally relevant teaching practices into our classrooms. Through the stories of our various projects, you'll see how we involved our students' families in our planning and teaching, recognizing them as valuable resources, having worthy knowledge. The examples we share show how we are surrounded by a plethora of human and material resources which are not just limited to our classroom libraries and the knowledge imparted from professional development.

If we want children to develop as successful learners, we must communicate that they belong in our classrooms. They need to see themselves, their cultures, their families, and their communities reflected in the materials and resources they find there. As culturally relevant teachers, we put the children we teach at the center of our practices.

WHY NOT? WHAT WORKS?

Understanding the Power, Possibility, and Effectiveness of Culturally Relevant and Responsive Teaching

MARIANA SOUTO-MANNING

"Education cannot be separated from the social, cultural, economic, and political context in which it happens." (Nieto 2010, 221)

As Carmen, Jessica, Abigail, and Alicia explained in Section 1, there is no such thing as acultural or neutral teaching (Freire 1970; Souto-Manning 2013). Curricular and instructional decisions are all cultural decisions (Au, Brown, and Calderón 2016; Delpit 1988; Freire 1970; Ladson-Billings 1995a, 1995b). What is included, excluded, and covered by the curriculum, what languages are valued, whose perspectives and voices are present or absent, whose histories are told and whose are silenced are all decisions resting on what those in power in our society deem important (Grant and Sleeter 1996).

In all subject areas, what we teach in schools is permeated with culture, and all curricula represent a particular way of seeing the world. For example, depending on where you grew up, you may think that the first pioneers to fly were the Wright Brothers . . . , or that Alberto Santos Dumont was the first. A common question such as "How many continents are there?" may result in different answers (all correct!) depending on your culture and upbringing. You may believe there are five continents (common in countries such as Brazil and Costa Rica) or seven (a common understanding in the United States). Instead of judging the answer as incorrect, it is important to understand that the knowledge students and their families have is *culturally situated*—not wrong.

The Mismatch of Culture and Curriculum

Students of color make up over 50 percent of the population in today's U.S. schools (National Center for Education Statistics 2014), and this percentage is expected to continue rising. Yet, adopted curricula rarely include or center on the histories and experiences of minoritized populations. I use the term *minoritized* instead of *minority* because "minority is stigmatizing and numerically inaccurate. . . . Minoritized more accurately conveys the power relations and processes by which certain groups are socially, economically, and politically marginalized within the larger society" (McCarty 2005, 48).

In many schools, the mismatch between the adopted curriculum and the student population it serves—like the kings and queens unit you read about in Section 1—fosters cultural injustice (Au 2014). Throughout history, "[s]cholars of color played major roles in contesting stereotypes and misconceptions about their groups by creating transformative and oppositional knowledge. . . . [and] constructed counternarratives and contested mainstream narratives that were detrimental to students and communities of color" (Banks 2016, 12).

Nevertheless, problems of errors, stereotypes, biases, and invisibility persist in curriculum and teaching today.

Learn how read-aloud can be a powerful tool for helping students see history from different perspectives in Section 3, page 70.

Although curriculum and teaching are always cultural, they are not always culturally relevant or responsive. Frequently, the official curriculum adopted by schools has factual errors, renders certain groups invisible, reinforces stereotypes, or tells just one side of a very complex story (e.g., Ahmed and Narcy-Combes 2011; Au, Brown, and Calderón 2016; Loewen 2007; Ndura 2004; Strauss 2014; Zinn 2007/2009, 2015). Historically and contemporarily, there have been errors of commission and omission, as verified by the Ontario Human Rights Commission (McDiarmit and Pratt 1971). Mel and Norma Gabler of Longview, Texas, through their organization, Educational Research Analysts (1997–2017), have pinpointed 249 factual errors in textbooks approved by Texas' Education Commissioner, including errors pertaining to result, narrative, provision, amendment, place, and event. For example, they explained: "The 15th Amendment did not guarantee suffrage to all citizens. It omitted women, making the 19th Amendment necessary," contrary to the statement included in *America: Pathways to the Present—Modern American History* (Cayton et al. 2007, 980).

A review of social studies textbooks commissioned by the Texas Freedom Network (2014) found that there are many problems related to cultural bias. Textbooks "include serious distortions of history and contemporary issues on topics ranging from religion and democracy to the free enterprise system and affirmative action, according to scholars" (Texas Freedom Network 2014). Here are four highlights from the findings shared by Valerie Strauss (2014) in *The Washington Post*:

- Several world history and world geography textbooks include biased statements that inappropriately portray Islam and Muslims negatively.

- Several world geography and history textbooks suffer from an incomplete—and often inaccurate—account of religions other than Christianity.
- A number of U.S. history textbooks evidence a general lack of attention to Native American peoples and culture and even include biased or misleading information.
- Most U.S. history textbooks do a poor job of covering the history of LGBT citizens in discussions of efforts to achieve civil rights in this country.

> **LGBT stands for Lesbian, Gay, Bisexual, and Transgender. It is a widely-used term. We prefer to use the term LGBTQIA+, as it includes queer, intersex, and asexual individuals and communities as well as many additional individuals and communities.**

And these examples are not the exception. James Banks (2016) explains that historically, textbooks forwarded the myth "that African Americans had not contributed significantly to the development of American history" (12). Brown and Au (2014) reviewed textbooks and found that they overwhelmingly tell the histories of White men. Minoritized populations, such as Native Americans and Chinese Americans, were portrayed from an inferiority or cultural deficit perspective (Au, Brown, and Calderón 2016; Goodwin et al. 2008; Valdés 1996).

According to Au, Brown, and Calderón (2016), the rich histories of communities from minoritized backgrounds are conspicuously absent from official curriculum and textbooks. "[C]urricular exclusion and revision have occurred in the United States. At the core of such exclusions has been the central location of Whiteness, where White histories and experiences were at the center of the educative and curricular process" (136). Whether or not this is an intentional exclusion, it has resulted in visible bias (Schubert 2010). Au, Brown, and Calderón (2016) explain that "the histories of official school curriculum" have impacted "the lives of young students of color" (16) negatively by "reproducing a kind of 'peculiar sensation,' an inexplicable feeling that one's life and experiences, histories, and knowledge are not valued" (16). They posit that as you "open the pages of textbooks and school curriculum," you "find out that your experiences are either nonexistent or presented in a manner that produces . . . 'amused contempt or pity.'" This "is unfortunately a perennial issue of schooling" (17).

Culturally irrelevant curriculum fosters monocultural competence—honoring and prioritizing one culture while excluding all others—and it can have serious consequences for all students including, but not limited to, those whose cultures are not represented. It cultivates White superiority and fosters prejudice.

Ignoring Culture in the Classroom Disadvantages Students

Ignoring the role of culture in teaching and curriculum effectively privileges the culture of power, sanctioning it as the standard against which performance, knowledge, and learning are measured. Researchers have documented this privileging for decades.

In the early eighties, Shirley Brice Heath published a ten-year ethnographic study of language use within and across Appalachian communities in North Carolina. In *Ways with Words: Language, Life, and Work in Communities and Classrooms* (1983), Heath documented how the interactional patterns of Black families differed from those of White families, and how schools advantaged White families by deeming their interactional patterns to be the appropriate and expected ways of interacting in school.

Kathryn Au (1980) documented how culturally appropriate instruction led to increased participation and achievement in a reading lesson. Specifically, she examined the role of talk story, "a major speech event in Hawaiian culture" (95), in fashioning culturally congruent participation structures for Hawaiian students. Au posited that "a context is inappropriate for a certain group of children if its construction violates their cultural norms," highlighting how "inappropriate contexts for learning may contribute to poor academic performance" (92).

In *Other People's Children: Cultural Conflict in the Classroom* (1995), Lisa Delpit analyzed her teaching, research, and experiences living in Papua New Guinea and Alaska, explaining how power imbalances and cultural conflicts within classrooms occur within a larger society that "nurtures and maintains stereotypes" (xii). She pinpointed the reluctance of people with power and privilege "to perceive those different from themselves except through their own culturally clouded vision" (xiv) as disempowering and problematic to teaching and learning. Her research showed how this is particularly destructive in classrooms where teachers view minoritized children as "damaged and dangerous caricatures of the vulnerable and impressionable beings before them" (xiii).

Guadalupe Valdés (1996) conducted a three-year ethnographic study of the familial expectations of ten first-generation Mexican working-class families living in "one of the Southwestern states bordering Mexico" (41) compared to those of U.S. schools. In *Con Respeto: Bridging the Distances Between Culturally Diverse Families and Schools*, she documented how functional behaviors (within these families' communities) were deemed inadequate or inappropriate by U.S. schoolteachers and how programs designed to educate parents and families often saw them and their children from deficit perspectives, not recognizing their rich practices, capacities, or funds of knowledge. These intervention programs were grounded in the belief "that children succeed in school only if their deficiencies are corrected and if they are taught to behave in more traditional mainstream ways in specially designed intervention programs" (17). This resulted from actions of well-meaning educators who "have decided to intervene and try to interrupt the pattern of failure" (33) without realizing how they were effectively enacting "an ideology of pathology" (Gutiérrez, Morales, and Martínez 2009, 227), as if they knew better than families how to raise, feed, and discipline children. The supposed problems of these minoritized families were defined without input from them and without an understanding of their rich cultural practices. Although teachers wanted "parents to support their children's school work," they were less interested "in parents' becoming genuinely involved . . . [beyond] their ability to help out as

For ideas about how to help families become *genuinely* involved in the classroom, see "Tapping into Funds of Knowledge" on page 66 of Section 3.

volunteers, as advocates of the school, and or as fundraisers" (38).

Valdés documented how parent education programs were designed to teach minoritized parents "how to be 'better' parents" (34) or "how to become 'good' parents" (192), but they focused on the cultural norms for child-rearing practices, appropriate nutrition, and desirable interactions with children that were not grounded in minoritized parents' practices, beliefs, or values. As interventions, most parent education programs presume to already know what is best, and they blame parents for systemic issues without acknowledging how the broader context encourages and fosters inequities. As such, parent education programs often result in resentment and distrust by minoritized parents. Furthermore, they do not acknowledge the different aims and purposes of education; on one hand, U.S. schools tend to position academic success as the pinnacle; on the other hand, the ten Mexican-American families from whom Valdés learned for three years primarily aimed to raise their children as good human beings. As she explains, reflecting on one of the mothers:

> If Rosario Castro . . . were made to believe that she should read to her children every evening, or listen to them read, or write stories, or practice multiplication tables, she would do just that. She is indeed committed to her children's schooling, and she would hope to do her best for them in spite of her many obligations. On the other hand, she would be replacing *educación* in the Mexican sense with an American middle-class focus on schooling and school learning. Given the demands on her life, she perhaps would not have the time to do the real teaching that Mexican mothers do. Her *consejos* [advice] would be hard to work into games, make-believe stories, and school recitations. In essence,

Rosario would be helping the teachers do their jobs, but she herself would fail to do her own. (Valdés 1996, 202–203)

Valdés (1996) helps us understand how educators' good intentions to intervene and to fix things and people can be damaging, especially because so many parent education programs are problematically grounded in the following assumption: "In an ideal world, new immigrants could be made into middle-class Americans in a series of parent education classes" (203). She highlights that we should not focus on replacing minoritized parent practices with middle-class ones through a series of workshops on how to _____ (fill in the blank with: feed your child, interact with your child, help your child).

In another three-year ethnographic study, Angela Valenzuela (1999) examined academic achievement and schooling as it related to Mexican and Mexican American students in a Houston, Texas, high school. She studied all of the school's 2,281 students through participant observation from 1992 to 1995. She also conducted a number of interviews with students, and examined student records and documents. In *Subtractive Schooling: U.S.-Mexican Youth and the Politics of Caring*, she reported finding that students were faring worse than previous generations of immigrants. For most of them, schooling was a subtractive process because it did not recognize the cultural resources of Mexican and Mexican American students, leaving them vulnerable to academic failure. Furthermore, she documented the lack of caring relationships between students and teachers; teachers did not see promise in students and did not have high expectations for them.

These and many other studies have documented that when children's cultural practices, images, and histories are absent from curriculum and teaching, children and families receive the message that their ways of being and behaving are not as important as the ways of those in power and they often become disengaged (e.g., Au, Brown, and Calderón 2016; Bishop 1990; Emdin 2016; Ladson-Billings 1994;

Nieto 2010; Souto-Manning 2010a; Souto-Manning and Martell 2016; Suárez-Orozco, Suárez-Orozco, and Todorova 2008; Tatum 1997; Villegas and Lucas 2002).

Mindset Shifts: Undoing Cultural Assumptions That Impact Teaching and Learning

Because teaching is never neutral, it goes without saying that assumptions—rooted in stereotypes—are often made about students based on their cultural identities. As Lisa Delpit explains (2012): "Without having the intention of discriminating, we do harm to children who are viewed within a stereotype of 'lesser than'" (6). How does this stereotype do harm? Delpit continues, "When we assume that certain children are less than brilliant . . . our tendency is to teach less, to teach down, to teach for remediation" (6). Unfortunately, research shows that certain assumptions frame how teachers view minoritized students and inevitably have an impact on teaching and learning. Rethinking these assumptions requires several mindset shifts.

> **Stereotypes lead to assumptions that impact teaching and learning.**

Move Away from "Saving Students"

One of the common explanations White teachers offer for wanting to teach and/or for teaching students of color is that they want to "save them" and help "those poor children." In such a way, they feel sorry for students before ever meeting them (Delpit 2012). Furthermore, by positioning themselves as saviors, they effectively vilify students, their families, and communities (Emdin 2016) and view students from a culturally deprived paradigm (Carter and Goodwin 2014). However well meaning, the assumption that students need to be saved is deeply problematic. Ladson-Billings (2001) explained how "'helping the less fortunate' can become a lens through which teachers see their role. . . . Such an approach to teaching diverse groups of students renders their culture irrelevant" (83).

What does it mean to shift this mindset? Teachers who engage in culturally relevant teaching "envision their students as being filled with possibilities. They imagine that somewhere in the classroom is the next Nobel laureate (a Toni Morrison)" (Ladson-Billings 2006b, 31). As teachers, we have to stop seeing students through lenses of "you poor dear" and view them through an assets-based lens, learning from and with students, their families, and communities, and working together for academic excellence. That is, we must recognize their brilliance, learning from them and acknowledging their giftedness (Hilliard 2009).

Challenge the Idea of a Race- or Culture-Based Achievement Gap

In the book *Multiplication Is for White People: Raising Expectations for Other People's Children*, Lisa Delpit (2012) invites us to question the idea of an inherent gap displayed by African American children. "Many reasons have been given for why African American children are not excelling in schools in the United States. One that is seldom spoken aloud, but that is buried within the American psyche, is that Black children are innately less capable—that they are somehow inferior" (3). The book then details a comparative review of pediatric research in African countries and the United States, where Delpit verified that there is no achievement gap that favors White European Americans—at least not at birth.

For example, in one study Delpit reviewed, researchers Geber and Dean "made a momentous discovery: despite the expectation that malnutrition would cause lower rates of infant development, the developmental rate of Ugandan infants was so much higher than the established norm that these babies were able to outperform European children twice or three times their age" (Delpit 2012, 3). They documented how in Uganda "four-day-old infants . . . smiled continuously" and "a forty-eight-hour child bolt upright, supported only by his forearms, head in perfect balance, and eyes focused" (3–4). The Geber and Dean study was published in 1957 in the academic journal *Pediatrics*, the official journal of the American Academy of Pediatrics, where the authors concluded, "Ugandan infants were months ahead of children of European descent on any intelligence scale utilized" (Delpit 2012, 4), including the Gesell test, developed at Yale University. Although most of these differences disappear by the time young children enter schooling (Geber and Dean 1958), they suggest that African American infants are not inferior or deprived as claimed by many.

The findings in Delpit's review contradicted many historical assumptions made by early childhood educators. As documented by Goodwin, Cheruvu, and Genishi (2008) in their review of research in the field of early childhood education, children of color have historically been framed as biologically inferior (as portrayed by studies that wrongfully claimed that the brains of African Americans were smaller than the brains of White European Americans), culturally deprived (not having the "proper" upbringing), and subsequently diverse (different from others). Such historical assumptions endure in schools and schooling practices. Yet some studies (Reyes, Scribner, and Scribner 1999; Lee 2007) show Latinx and African American students thriving academically within and across settings. These studies reposition students from minoritized backgrounds, recognizing their promise and suggesting ways schooling can contribute to the full realization of their academic and human potential. Findings like these challenge us to take responsibility for our actions in the creation of a racialized achievement gap. They beg for a mindset shift because, as Delpit (2012) concludes, if "we do not recognize the brilliance before us, we cannot help but carry on the stereotypic societal views that these children are somehow damaged goods and that they cannot be expected to succeed" (5).

Rewrite the Metaphor for Achievement: It's a Debt, Not a Gap!

The assumption that an "achievement gap" explains how minoritized children of color and low-income children fall behind in school reinforces the idea of individual deficits and ignores social responsibility for schooling and societal inequities (Ladson-Billings 2006a). In her American Educational Research Association Presidential Lecture, Gloria Ladson-Billings (2006a) explored the history of educational inequities through an economic lens and proposed that we have a debt in education, not a gap. Although a gap is a year-to-year budget deficit, a debt is year after year of accumulated deficits; so even if the budget is balanced one year and there is no deficit, there is still a debt accumulated historically. Year after year, funding inequities, poor health services, political exclusion, and other deficits have created a debt in education (Ladson-Billings 2010).

Making a mindset shift from thinking of *gaps* to thinking of *debts* is critical because "the debt language holds us all accountable. When we talk about the gap, we say 'those kids, those schools, those teachers;' when we talk about national debt, we all ask: 'What's my part in this? How much do I owe?' So education debt throws it back on all of us. It leads us to ask: 'What should I be doing?'" (Ladson-Billings 2010). Culturally relevant teaching can serve as a pathway for teachers to address this education debt in their own classrooms, instead of blaming students and their families for how they are being failed by schooling and by society.

Reposition Culture as Additive, Not Subtractive

When the U.S. Supreme Court ruled in *Brown v. Board of Education* (1954), it established that separate education was not equal, creating legal grounds for the racial integration of schools. In the decades that followed, education researchers sought to desegregate curriculum as well as buildings and to integrate not only racialized bodies, but bodies of knowledge and interactional norms (Aronson and Laughter 2016; Sleeter 2012). Over time, these researchers have become increasingly critical of "culture" as an impediment to learning (McDermott and Varenne 1995; Valdés 1996).

Refuting the claim that minoritized individuals are culturally inferior or deprived, and recognizing the value of cultural diversities (Goodwin, Cheruvu, and Genishi 2008), a number of researchers have urged schools to rethink curriculum and teaching in culturally inclusive and racially just ways. Moll and colleagues (1992) called on teachers and schools to document, value, and reposition family funds of knowledge, moving beyond stereotypes and valuing family expertise. As Sonia Nieto (2013) explains, "Teaching is honoring students' identities and believing in their futures" (130).

> **Honoring students' identities begins with learning to pronounce their names.**
>
> See Section 3, page 54.

Engaging in teaching that honors culture starts with making curriculum more inclusive of multiple perspectives and points of view.

Many researchers have documented the power of pedagogies that build on students' strengths and foster cultural competence (for example, Ladson-Billings 1994; González, Moll, and Amanti 2005; Souto-Manning 2013). These researchers have not proposed that we replace one truth with another, but that we recognize that each of us teaches from a certain perspective. Research invites us to question and move past single stories which exclude many students (Adichie 2009), and instead find "joy in teaching students from diverse backgrounds" (Nieto 2013).

Defining Culturally Relevant and Responsive Teaching

The question, of course, is what all of this looks like in the classroom. In a synthesis of research on culturally relevant education, Brittany

Aronson and Judson Laughter (2016) identified two primary strands that have emerged. One strand is focused on teacher practice and is embodied by the work of Geneva Gay (1975, 1980, 2002, 2010, 2013). The second strand is focused on teacher mindset and cultural understanding—what Aronson and Laughter call "postures and paradigms"—and is best expressed in the work of Gloria Ladson-Billings (1994, 1995a, 1995b, 2006b, 2014). Together the two strands consider both actions and beliefs and form a powerful framework for understanding culturally relevant teaching.

Culturally Responsive Teaching: A Focus on Teacher Practice

Geneva Gay (2010) defined "culturally responsive teaching" as "using the cultural knowledge, prior experiences, frames of reference and performance styles of ethnically diverse students to make learning encounters more relevant to and effective for them" (31). In her work, Gay identified six key practices of culturally responsive teaching:

- having high expectations for all students
- engaging students' cultural knowledges, experiences, practices, and perspectives
- bridging gaps between home and school practices
- seeking to educate the whole child
- identifying and leveraging students' strengths to transform education
- critically questioning normative schooling practices, content, and assessments.

Engaging in these practices requires a shift in mindset: interrupting and disrupting deficit perspectives and subtractive conceptions of students from minoritized backgrounds, their families, and their communities (Gay 2013). Culturally responsive teaching means including multiple perspectives in the curriculum and engaging in critical reviews and revisions of what is in place. Teachers who engage in these practices understand the importance of culture to teaching, learning, growing, and developing—what Rogoff (2003) called the cultural nature of human development. Finally, Gay made clear that teaching that is culturally responsive must be situated within a particular context, meaningful to the members of the learning community.

Culturally Relevant Pedagogy: A Focus on Teacher Mindset and Cultural Understanding

Gloria Ladson-Billings studied a group of eight successful teachers of African American children. Three of these teachers were White and five were African American. They were all able to engage African American students in meaningful ways, resulting in high-level academic performance, despite the odds and the resources available to them. Ladson-Billings (1994, 1995a, 1995b, 2009) used the term *culturally relevant pedagogy* to describe what she observed in these classrooms—the kind of teaching that views children of color as being "at promise" instead of "at risk" (Swadener and Lubeck 1995).

The teaching styles of these eight teachers were very different, but in the first edition of *The Dreamkeepers: Successful Teachers of African American Children* (1994), Ladson-Billings documented how they all had the same laserlike focus on three things:

1. student learning
2. cultural competence
3. critical consciousness.

Later, the second edition of *Dreamkeepers* (2009) featured a number of newer (less experienced) teachers from a variety of contexts and backgrounds. The teaching styles of this group were also very different, but their teaching was guided by a belief in students as capable, a commitment to foster cultural competence, and a critical stance, which helped them question injustices in schooling and society. With these studies, Ladson-Billings showed that teachers' mindsets and cultural understandings make a big difference in whether teaching is culturally relevant or not.

Make the Move to Culturally Relevant Teaching

In Section 3, Carmen, Jessica, Abigail, and Alicia will show you what culturally relevant teaching looks like in each of their diverse classrooms. But first, let's consider some guiding principles—supported by research—for the teaching you will read about there.

Student Learning

Student learning, or what we often think of as academic achievement, may appear to be an obvious tenet of teaching, but much of what happens in classrooms focuses on what teachers cover rather than on student learning. When we think of teaching, we often think about the curriculum . . . about coverage. We may also think of a high rate of failure as evidence of rigor. At the 2014 John M. Wozniak Lecture Series at Loyola University Chicago, Gloria Ladson-Billings challenged this focus in an address titled "Getting Serious About Education: Culturally Relevant Teaching for New Century Students" (2014). The author and researcher issued a call for teachers and schools to focus on the students we teach instead of being concerned about curriculum coverage; to focus on depth and on mastery; to focus on learning rather than on teaching. The focus must be on students—on their learning, not on how fast or slow we can go through the lessons in a mandated guide. Not just student test scores, but on a full "range of what young people learn."

> **Culturally relevant practices are student-centered and focus on what is being learned rather than what is being covered.**

In the address, Ladson-Billings used a powerful metaphor to explain the need to refocus. She pinpointed how many teachers see their classes as a sieve through which their students must pass-by memorizing their teachers' thoughts and beliefs. In this way, students are positioned passively, as recipients of knowledge. Culturally relevant teaching requires moving away from this and positioning students as producers of knowledge and our classes as nets which support their learning. There are incredible learning possibilities when students are engaged as creators and producers rather than as consumers and recipients.

Finally, Ladson-Billings challenged teachers and schools to abandon the notion of high failure as equating quality teaching or as a desirable characteristic of teaching, embracing rigor instead. We should demand a high level of performance, she said, while also providing a high level of support. As you'll see documented in Section 3, culturally relevant teaching is not about differentiating or tweaking the traditional content, but about reimagining education in racially and culturally just ways.

Employing Ladson-Billings' culturally relevant pedagogy as a framework, Morrison, Robbins, and Rose (2008) reviewed forty-five classroom-based research studies in the United States and internationally, finding that teachers who taught in culturally relevant ways supported student learning while having high expectations through:

- engaging in modeling, scaffolding, and the clarification of curricular expectations
- positioning students' strengths at the center of curriculum and teaching
- investing in and taking responsibility for students' success
- fostering a nurturing and collaborative learning community
- communicating and enacting high behavioral and academic expectations.

But—what does this look like? How do high academic expectations with a high level of support manifest themselves in practice?

As Hanley and Noblit (2009) affirmed, "There is literature that suggests that culturally responsive [and relevant] approaches contribute to positive racial identity, resiliency and achievement" (52). The following classroom-based studies documented the impact of supporting student learning (note that none embody *all* of the operationalized ways of supporting student learning listed previously).

Engaging in Modeling, Scaffolding, and the Clarification of Curricular Expectations

To support student learning while upholding high expectations, researchers have documented the benefits of engaging in clarifying, modeling, and scaffolding curricular expectations. Specifically, modeling metacognitive strategies and providing scaffolding are ways teachers can operationalize high learning expectations (Morrison, Robbins, and Rose 2008). Cahnmann and Remillard's (2002) qualitative study of two third-grade teachers in an urban setting, focusing on culturally, linguistically, and socioeconomically diverse students, shows us how modeling metacognitive strategies, collaboration, and scaffolding improved students' mathematical achievement. The teachers specifically engaged in making cultural connections with students and offering meaningful and complex mathematics problems. Drawing on these teachers' practices, Cahnmann and Remillard offer a framework that builds on the fields of mathematics and bilingual/bicultural education, combining high expectations with culturally relevant teaching practices.

Learn how students can create their own culturally relevant texts through collaborative bookmaking.

See Section 3, page 59.

Jiménez's (1997) qualitative study provides insights into how specific cognitive strategy lessons for reading led to increased literacy achievement among middle school Latinx multilingual learners. Specifically, Jiménez inquires into the teaching of strategies to middle school multilingual learners using unknown vocabulary, prior knowledge, and questioning. He sought to understand how five students deemed to have low literacy responded to cognitive strategy instruction. He found that students participated in strategy lessons that involved culturally relevant texts and used their home languages to support comprehension (through the use of cognates, translation, and other moves). Instead of seeing the students as having no language, leveraging students' existent linguistic repertoires allowed them to develop expertise.

Positioning Students' Strengths at the Center of Curriculum and Teaching

Researchers have documented the need for students of color to see themselves in the texts they read and in their teachers, who effectively position their strengths and experiences as relevant and integral (Bell and Clark 1998; Bishop 1990; Feger 2006; Morrison, Robbins, and Rose 2008; Souto-Manning and Martell 2016). For example, Bell and Clark (1998) conducted a quantitative study identifying the positive effects of using culturally relevant texts and making expectations clear to African American elementary-aged students. They examined the effects of racial images and cultural themes on the reading comprehension of African American children in first to fourth grade. They found that "comprehension was significantly more efficient for stories depicting both Black imagery and culturally related themes than for stories depicting both White imagery and culturally distant themes" (470). Feger (2006) conducted a teacher research study and found that the use of culturally relevant literature increased student engagement in high school Spanish for native speakers (ninth and tenth grades), finding that books deemed to be culturally relevant increased students' desire to read.

Investing in and Taking Responsibility for Students' Success

Teachers can communicate high expectations through investments in student learning (Ladson-Billings 1994, 1995a, 1995b). One way of doing so is by taking responsibility for students' success by learning about their cultural and linguistic strengths, and (re)positioning them at the center of teaching. This serves to support and leverage student learning in culturally relevant ways (Hollie 2001; Jiménez and Gertsen 1999; Morrison, Robbins, and Rose 2008; Souto-Manning 2013). Brokering the code of schooling and bridging home and school communicative practices are important components of operationalizing high academic expectations. For example, Jiménez and Gertsen (1999) conducted a qualitative study (drawing on extensive observations and interviews) that documented student learning with a focus on how two Latinx teachers' influences on instruction (including rapport, language, and culture) positively influenced the academic achievement of Latinx students in the elementary grades (specifically related to literacy). They affirmed that "it is not so much shared ethnicity as shared cultural and social norms that influence the educational success of minority students" (296). The teachers established strong rapport with students, which served as the basis for engaging in culturally relevant teaching and resulted in literacy gains.

Hollie's (2001) observational study identified clear expectations as an effective strategy teachers used to help African American students acquire the language of power (identified by the researcher as "Standard American English") while maintaining African American Language through the "Linguistic Affirmation Program . . . a comprehensive nonstandard language awareness program designed to serve the needs of . . . students who are not proficient in Standard American English" (54). The program had six key instructional approaches, which, when combined, improved writing for multilingual learners, further developing their knowledge of dominant American English (the so-called "Standard English Language"):

- Reconceptualize teachers' knowledge and attitude regarding multilingual learners, their families, and communities.
- Reposition African American Language and other minoritized languages in teaching.
- Use multilingualism and translanguaging methodologies.

- Employ balanced and culturally-grounded approaches to literacy.
- Design teaching grounded in the strengths of multilingual learners.
- Infuse the history of multiple languages—e.g., dominant American English, African American Language—and languaging practices in curriculum and teaching.

Fostering a Nurturing and Collaborative Learning Community

Fostering a nurturing learning community that reflects minoritized students' cultural values is also important in supporting student learning (Morrison, Robbins, and Rose 2008; Stuart and Volk 2002). Stuart and Volk conducted a qualitative study of peer collaboration and the use of culturally relevant texts in a summer literacy program for six- to eight-year-olds (most of whom were Spanish-English bilinguals of Puerto Rican heritage), documenting literacy gains. The curriculum built on children's home experiences. The children collaborated in discussion (e.g., brainstorming prior to reading), reading (e.g., paired reading), writing (e.g., journal writing, mapping stories), and project extensions (e.g., acting out stories, creating puppets). A teacher reported: "The more I had incorporated culturally relevant literature . . . the more my students' engagement in reading had increased" (18). Stuart and Volk suggest that by fostering collaboration, teachers acknowledge that there is more expertise distributed in the classroom learning community than in any one particular individual, a hallmark of culturally relevant teaching (Ladson-Billings 2012).

Communicating and Enacting High Expectations

Finally, having high expectations and genuinely believing that students will succeed are key (Gutiérrez 2000; Morrison, Robbins, and Rose 2008; Sheets 1995). This involves acknowledging, cultivating, and sustaining their promise (Swadener and Lubeck 1995). High expectations can make a critical difference even for older students who may not have always experienced them in earlier years of schooling. They must be communicated and enacted in curriculum and teaching.

In a teacher research study, Sheets (1995) documented student learning and the positive effects of challenging students in remedial Spanish class to take Advanced Placement (AP) Spanish exams through an advanced Spanish class for speakers of Spanish as a heritage language. The class was not restricted to textbook knowledge and grammatical concepts applied to reading and writing, but was grounded in conversations through literature and culture. This allowed students to see themselves as capable and their Spanish language repertoire to be recognized as an asset. They leveraged their verbal dexterity for deeper learning, and although Sheets explained that the AP test was difficult, she communicated to the students and their families her belief that they could succeed. Each of the five Spanish-speaking students had failed a Spanish 2 class; yet, in advanced Spanish, they flourished and passed AP Spanish exams with scores of 4 and 5 (earning at least 10 college credits). The students performed according to their teacher's high expectations.

Gutiérrez's (2000) qualitative study (drawing on interviews, questionnaires, analysis of school documents, and school observations) of high school African American students in advanced math documents the centrality of teacher modeling, scaffolding, and of teachers taking personal responsibility for students' success. With a rigorous curriculum, students experienced academic success because of the active commitment of their teachers: they were accessible outside of class, engaged in tutoring, had positive views of students, and understood learning as dynamic. The teachers were willing to teach a range of courses so they would know more of the students, engaged in collective problem solving and collaboration, and shared resources relevant to students' lives. High expectations and high support allowed the students "to perform well on standardized tests and to display high rates of participation in the mathematics curriculum" (102).

Culturally relevant materials are important, but it's teachers who really make the difference in students' success.

Cultural Competence

In *Belonging, Being & Becoming: The Early Years Learning Framework for Australia* (Commonwealth of Australia 2009), cultural competence is defined as the ability to understand, communicate with, and effectively interact with people across cultures. Cultural competence encompasses:

- being aware of one's own worldview
- developing positive attitudes toward cultural differences
- gaining knowledge of different cultural practices and world views
- developing skills for communication and interaction across cultures (16).

Ladson-Billings (1995b) defines cultural competence as "the dynamic and synergistic relationship between home/community culture and school culture" (467). This encompasses the development of positive ethnic, racial, and cultural identities. She underscores that students should not be forced to undergo a process of cultural erasure to succeed academically.

Cultural competence, of course, is important to any person in any field of work, but it is especially critical in teaching. Ladson-Billings (1995a) contends: "Culturally relevant teachers utilize students' culture as a vehicle for learning" (161). Culturally competent teaching is built on the premise that it is essential for teachers to know as much as possible about the cultures of the children and youth they teach. Teachers must commit to deep and rigorous studies of their students' cultures and histories so they're able to plan in culturally relevant ways. "Teachers who foster cultural competence understand that they must work back and forth between the lives of their students and the life of school" (Ladson-Billings 2006b, 36). Thus, it is important to learn from students' families and communities—not to develop assumptions and judgments, but to expand our own outlook on the world. This requires recognizing that teaching and learning occur within and across multiple social contexts—classrooms, schools, families, and communities (Ladson-Billings 2006b). Yet, "when it comes to cultural competence, good intentions have not translated into good practice" (Leonardo and Grubb 2014, 70).

As noted earlier, Brittany Aronson and Judson Laughter (2016) reviewed more than forty studies related to culturally relevant education. In their synthesis of the research, the importance of cultural competence in the classroom was clear. They note:

> Students in every content area made connections to academic cultures and gained pride in their home cultures through developing connections between the two. In math, students gained power and agency to solve problems. In science, students came to value multiple ways of creating knowledge. In history/social studies, students upended discourses of invisibility. In ELA [English language arts], students saw language as a medium for connecting across cultures. (198)

Culturally competent teaching comes to life as teachers critically recenter and reshape the prescribed curriculum, making it fully inclusive of historically marginalized and minoritized perspectives. It also comes to life through the documentation of students', families', and communities' funds of knowledge (more on that later), which are leveraged to enrich teaching and learning. Finally, it comes to life through cultivating authentic relationships and developing horizontal partnerships between schools and communities, in which schools reject notions of power *over* and develop power *with* families and communities (Morrison, Robbins, and Rose 2008). Culturally competent teachers exist across gender, race, ethnicity, experience, background, and geography (Ladson-Billings 2009). Yet, they all recognize that their students are "a group of students from whom they can learn" (Ladson-Billings 2012).

Understanding Your Own Culture

The first step to developing cultural competence is understanding how *you* are a cultural being (Souto-Manning 2013). This may sound simple, yet it requires understanding that ways of being and behaving in the world are culturally situated and power-laden. Thus, no individual, family, or community should be regarded as "normal." After all, this label cloaks the interests of dominant groups in society (Scribner 1970). Based on her study of preservice and beginning teachers, Ladson-Billings (2001) affirmed: "The average white teacher has no idea what it feels like to be a numerical or political minority in the classroom. The persuasiveness of whiteness makes the experience of most teachers the accepted norm" (81).

To begin to understand who you are as a cultural being, consider the following questions:

- What cultural threads make up the fabric of who I am?
- What aspects of my identity afford me privileges?
- What are the racial and linguistic backgrounds of those who surround me in school/at work? What does this tell me?
- What assumptions do outsiders associate with me? What do these assumptions tell me about the privileges and oppressions I experience?
- Do I see and actively question inequities that exist in the (pre) schools where I work?

(Souto-Manning 2013, 19)

Understanding yourself as a cultural being is the first step in recognizing that every one of your students is a unique cultural being. This recognition will help you avoid making problematic and faulty assumptions that might disadvantage students whose backgrounds are different from your own. And even if you are a lot *like* your students in terms of culture, it's important not to presume that you already know what any one student is like (Ladson-Billings 2012). There is great diversity within cultural groups, and cultural competence does not mean applying a simplistic single story of a culture to an entire group of people. After all, single stories foster stereotypes—not because they are not true, but because they are partial. It is thus important to understand that any single story is not the only story about an entire cultural group (Adichie 2009).

In addition to being firmly grounded in your own culture, it's important for both you *and* your students to be fluent in at least one other culture. Despite the ways in which schools currently (re)present other groups' histories and cultures marginally or as electives, Ladson-Billings posited that "White middle class students are not exempt from developing cultural competence. And although schools generally cater to their culture, they too need to be fluent in at least one other culture" (Ladson-Billings 2014). All students can and should leave schools multiculturally competent.

Tapping into Funds of Knowledge

A second important step in becoming culturally competent is recognizing that *your students* are cultural beings and each of them—as members of families and communities—has rich funds of knowledge. Funds of knowledge are "the historically accumulated and culturally developed bodies of knowledge and skills essential for household or individual functioning and well-being" (Moll et al. 1992, 133). Every child in every classroom has rich funds of knowledge they can access. As teachers committed to culturally relevant teaching, we must identify, cultivate, leverage, and sustain minoritized students', families', and communities' funds of knowledge. For example, teacher Marla Hensley (2005) found that regardless of the widespread perception that families in the Tucson, Arizona, neighborhood where she teaches "are viewed as lacking" (143), they have multiple funds of knowledge—such as gardening, quilting, and music (guitar-playing, singing, composing, etc.). Culturally competent teachers recognize that there is more expertise in the families and communities that surround the classroom than there is within its walls. They commit to studying families and communities, learning about their expertise, and documenting funds of knowledge (Moll et al. 1992).

Funds of knowledge serve as "extended zones of proximal development" (Moll and Greenberg 1990, 344) and invite educators to journey beyond the classroom walls to unveil the rich and varied cultural resources of students, families, and communities. Not as experts, but as learners. That is, educators must position themselves as ethnographers, studying their students' cultures and acknowledging the resources they have, learning about their strengths and brilliance. This allows us educators to abandon the oft-perceived deficits which have typically shaped the way members of minoritized communities are positioned/viewed.

> **Skillful interviewing is a great tool for tapping into funds of knowledge. See how Jessica teaches her students this in Section 3, page 66.**

In *Funds of Knowledge: Theorizing Practices in Households, Communities and Classrooms*, editors Norma González, Luis Moll, and Cathy Amanti (2005) share how they learned about their students' lives outside school through household visits and neighborhood studies. Once teachers entered students' homes, they "asked respectful questions and learned to listen to answers" (10). Chapter authors document how students' funds of knowledge were then leveraged in teaching and learning, generating new understandings and a culturally relevant curriculum. For example, teacher Martha Floyd Tenery (2005) engaged in home visits to learn about family funds of knowledge related to home remedies and navigating within and across the United States and Mexico (tourism, taxes, and international commerce), positioning them as foundations for teaching units she developed. Teacher Cathy Amanti (2005) gained firsthand knowledge of her students and their extensive knowledge of horses, positioning horses at the center of her teaching, which was "not about replicating what students have learned at home, but about using students' knowledge and prior experiences as a scaffold for new learning" (135), rendering their family funds of knowledge "academically valid" (138).

When we teachers believe that there is something *worth* learning about the students we teach, their families, and their communities, we're forced to cross "the lines of strangeness" (Bateson 2000, quoted in González 2005, 29) and learn both from and with them, while also seeing and critically examining ourselves as cultural beings with unique cultural perspectives, experiences, and assumptions. Culturally competent teachers "know that students who have the academic and cultural wherewithal to succeed in school without losing their identities are better prepared to be of service to others; in a democracy, this commitment to the public good is paramount" (Ladson-Billings 2001, 97).

Critical Consciousness

According to Ladson-Billings (2012), critical consciousness is about helping students "understand that their learning can and should be connected to the everyday problems of living in a society that is deeply divided along racial, ethnic, linguistic, economic, environmental, social, political, and cultural lines." Through the development of critical consciousness, students develop an awareness that education can and should be leveraged in critical ways to alleviate societal inequities and injustices. According to Gay (2010), critical consciousness engages students' cultural knowledge, experiences, practices, and perspectives and leads them to name and question issues of inequity and injustice in their lives. Souto-Manning (2010a) defines critical consciousness as "critical meta-awareness" (42), which includes the critical consideration of multiple perspectives and the problematization of inequities and injustices in schooling and in society. Critical consciousness is the "so what?" of culturally relevant teaching.

> **Story acting can help students develop the empathy and understanding necessary for critical consciousness.**
>
> See Section 3, page 73.

In their synthesis of classroom-based research, Morrison, Robbins, and Rose (2008) explain that critical consciousness is operationalized in classrooms through four practices: using critical literacy, engaging students in social justice work, making the power dynamics in society explicit to students, and sharing power in the classroom.

Using Critical Literacy

In addition to embodying a critical stance themselves, teachers help students problematize what they read—in texts and in their worlds— inviting them to delve in between the lines and beyond face value, unveiling structural inequities and injustices. Teachers select texts that offer multiple points of view and critical perspectives. Additionally, they provide critical invitations prior to reading a text (for students to consider inequities and issues of power). Finally, instead of avoiding controversial issues, they create spaces for students to delve into controversial topics, problematizing injustices in schooling and in society.

Engaging Students in Social Justice Work

Beyond critical readings of texts, culturally relevant teachers foster critical consciousness by engaging students in reflections leading to action— "Now that you know about these inequities, what will you do?" and "How will you lead by example?" They design learning experiences that allow students to unveil inequities (e.g., lack of access to fresh produce due to availability and price variance across neighborhoods being closely tied to income). As a result, "[s]tudents also engaged in social justice work by providing real services to their community" (Morrison, Robbins, and Rose 2008, 442) and by rethinking their own actions. For example, Parsons (2005) documented how one White teacher engaged students in disrupting patterns of talk in which White students silenced African American students, thereby interrupting injustice.

Making the Power Dynamics in Society Explicit to Students

Culturally relevant teachers do not pretend that meritocracy exists and that students can ascend the social and economic ladders through hard work. Instead, they recognize that there is a culture of power, which is defined by those who have power. Instead of deeming such cultural practices better, culturally relevant teachers validate and value minoritized students' cultural practices, cultivating and sustaining them, while helping students become fluent in the language and culture of power. They value students' cultural and communicative repertoires and purposefully do not condone processes of cultural and linguistic erasure—all while remaining "cognizant of the need to prepare students for participation in the dominant culture of power" (Morrison, Robbins, and Rose 2008, 443).

Sharing Power in the Classroom

Instead of enacting the role of teacher as sole expert and decision maker in the classroom, culturally relevant teachers blur the traditional roles of teacher and learner (Freire 1998). They engage students in deciding on classroom values and practices, developing curriculum cogeneratively (Emdin 2016), and employing culturally valid assessments. Culturally relevant teachers regard their students as capable and position their expertise centrally.

To foster critical consciousness in their teaching, teachers must develop "a sociopolitical consciousness of their own" (Ladson-Billings 2006b, 37). Ladson Billings (2006b) explains that "the first thing teachers must do is educate themselves about both the local sociopolitical issues of their school community . . . and the larger sociopolitical issues (e.g., unemployment, health care, housing) that impinge upon their students' lives" (37). Then, they must (re)position such sociopolitical issues centrally in their curriculum and teaching. In doing so, teachers can help students critique, problematize, and better understand injustices in schooling and within society. That is, instead of shying away from issues of inequity and injustice, culturally relevant teachers (re) position them front and center in their classrooms. After all, culturally relevant teaching requires us to see teaching for justice as an ethical imperative we must take on and not just something we do.

The Effectiveness of Culturally Relevant Teaching Across Content Areas

Is culturally relevant teaching effective? Yes! In 2012, Sleeter stated that the marginalization of culturally relevant teaching is not due to its lack of power, but because (a) there are overly simplistic notions of what culturally relevant teaching is, (b) there is too little research connecting culturally relevant teaching to traditional measures of student achievement, and (c) there is resistance to doing away with the normalization of White ways of being and behaving in curriculum and teaching, a "fear of losing national and global hegemony" (562). She underscored "a clear need for evidence-based research that documents connections between culturally responsive pedagogy and student outcomes" (578).

Aronson and Laughter (2016) responded to Sleeter's call by reviewing over forty studies (both qualitative and quantitative). They found that culturally relevant teaching is effective—while acknowledging that the studies they reviewed offered varying degrees of evidence. In the review, Aronson and Laughter expanded student outcome to include traditional student achievement as well as other components of student success—namely, motivation, empowerment, critical discourse, and agency. They showed evidence of the effectiveness of culturally relevant teaching in mathematics, science, social studies, and English/language arts. The authors affirmed: "No matter the outcome discussed, the research demonstrates that the engagement of . . . [culturally relevant teaching] across the content areas resulted in positive increases in academic skills and concepts" (196). The chart on page 47 highlights a few studies that link culturally relevant teaching to student achievement across academic areas.

Engaging in Culturally Relevant Teaching

Ladson-Billings (2006a) argued "that teachers engaged in culturally relevant pedagogy must be able to deconstruct, construct, and reconstruct" the curriculum, problematizing and taking apart official knowledge to "expose its weaknesses, myths, distortions, and omissions."

Culturally Relevant Teaching in Specific Academic Contexts

Language and Literacy

Bui and Fagen (2013): A quasi-experimental study involving forty-nine fifth-grade students, which evaluated the effects of the Integrated Reading Comprehension Strategy with and without multicultural literature and cooperative learning, using a pretest-posttest design. Pre- and posttests measured students' reading levels and had three independent variables: word recognition, reading comprehension, and story retell. Findings support culturally relevant teaching—connecting the school's teaching and learning environment with students' personal and cultural experiences, leading to increased achievement, engagement, and motivation.

Mathematics

Mitescu and colleagues (2011): A quantitative study using the Teaching for Social Justice Observation Scale to examine the extent to which twenty-two novice elementary teachers implemented mathematics teaching practices grounded in social justice. It documented gains in student outcomes as measured by end-of-unit district-based assessments. The study found a significant, positive relationship between teaching for social justice and student outcomes ($r = 0.44$, $P < 0.05$).

Science

Roehrig and colleagues (2011): A mixed-methods study on the impact of long-term culturally relevant professional development for Head Start teachers focusing on the teaching of science through inquiry within the context of an American Indian Reservation. Findings indicate that Classroom Assessment Scoring System (CLASS) scores increased in statistically significant ways as teachers' classroom practices became more culturally relevant and inquiry based.

Social Studies

Coughran (2012): Teacher action research in a kindergarten classroom, fostering culturally relevant teaching through two twenty-minute social studies lessons per week over two months. This was part of a multicultural social studies unit aiming to alleviate the presence of stereotype threat and reject deficit attitudes being attributed to people of color. Analyzing videos of lessons, reflections, and interviews with eight students, Coughran found that connecting students' lived experiences to the curriculum increased their understanding of racism. Culturally relevant social studies lessons also strengthened her relationship with her students.

As you saw in Section 1, Carmen, Jessica, Abigail, and Alicia understand that any curriculum is a cultural artifact shaped by the culture of power. It is never neutral. The vignettes in that section show how "some of the pedagogical strategies that make teaching easier or more convenient . . . may be exactly the kind of instruction [teachers] should avoid" (Ladson-Billings 2006b, 33).

What does it mean to engage in culturally relevant teaching? What does it look like? In Section 3, Carmen, Jessica, Abigail, and Alicia show you how they honor, cultivate, leverage, and sustain the cultural practices, rich experiences, and historical legacies minoritized students bring to the classroom. These are centrally positioned in their teaching. In doing so, they engage in reconstructing the curriculum after taking it apart and problematizing its biases, silences, and inequities. With regard to curriculum, they know that it is "never enough to tear it down. Teachers must be prepared to build up and fill in the holes that emerge when students begin to use critical analysis as they attempt to make sense of the curriculum" (Ladson-Billings 2006b, 32). Carmen, Jessica, Abigail, and Alicia also know that no curriculum can come to life on its own or teach itself.

As you turn the page and start reading Section 3, you will see a wide repertoire of teaching strategies and approaches—interviews, story acting, funds of knowledge, inquiry—come to life across diverse classroom contexts. In sharing their stories of teaching, Carmen, Jessica, Abigail, and Alicia take up Sleeter's (2012) call for "the need to educate parents, teachers, and education leaders about what culturally responsive pedagogy means and looks like in the classroom" (578). The rich and varied practices they share allows students to access the curriculum, making teaching culturally relevant, and fostering educational success. They shed light on the power, possibility, and imperative of culturally relevant teaching.

Resources—from Classic to Contemporary —to Help You Understand the Importance of Cultural Relevance in Teaching

Bishop, R. S. 1990. "Mirrors, Windows, and Sliding Glass Doors." *Perspectives* **6 (3): ix–xi.**

Bishop explains that children must see themselves in classroom texts. These texts can affirm minoritized students' identities and practices, and communicate belonging. Reading can become "a means of self-affirmation" if readers find "mirrors in books" (ix); yet, children of color often learn to read words and worlds in books which erase, silence, and marginalize them. This can be academically and socioemotionally damaging.

Ladson-Billings, G. 1994. *The Dreamkeepers: Successful Teachers of African American Children.* **San Francisco, CA: Jossey-Bass.**

Ladson-Billings documents the culturally relevant practices of eight teachers with distinct teaching styles, each of whom created intellectually rigorous and challenging classrooms where students could see their images, values, and cultural practices in curriculum and teaching. All of these teachers had high expectations for their students, fostered cultural competence, and engaged in the development of critical consciousness.

Tatum, B. D. 1997. *"Why Are All The Black Kids Sitting Together in the Cafeteria?" and Other Conversations About Race.* **New York: Basic Books.**

Tatum explores the racially divided landscape of U.S. schools and explains how straight talk about students' racial identities—and about our own—is essential if we are to engage in education across historically established racial and ethnic divides. She clarifies how processes of racial identity development are entangled in learning.

Resources (*continues*)

Villegas, A. M., and T. Lucas. 2002. *Educating Culturally Responsive Teachers: A Coherent Approach*. Albany, NY: State University of New York Press.

The authors explain how "'remedial' practices devalue the individual and cultural strengths that students from nondominant groups bring to school, produce low-academic outcomes, and promote a sense of alienation and disempowerment among these children" (39). They also make visible how the overwhelming absence of teachers of color deprives the ever-growing population of students of color of role models, cultural brokers, and advocates.

Suárez-Orozco, C., M. Suárez-Orozco, and I. Todorova. 2008. *Learning in a New Land: Immigrant Students in American Society*. Cambridge, MA: Harvard University Press.

Drawing on data collected in Boston and San Francisco, the authors studied hundreds of immigrant students, ages nine to fourteen. They highlight the importance of linguistic, cultural, and emotional ties in student learning, with families as well as with peers and teachers; the important role of mentors; and some of the obstacles tied to stereotypical and overly simplistic images ascribed to these students.

Nieto, S. 2010. *The Light in Their Eyes: Creating Multicultural Learning Communities*. 10th Anniversary Ed. New York: Teachers College Press.

Nieto explains how culture extends beyond foods and folklore to include daily practices and lived experiences. Children experience cultural practices in situated and relational ways, grounded in their families' values, and schools must honor these cultural practices in order to create truly multicultural learning communities.

Souto-Manning, M. 2010. "Teaching English Learners: Building on Cultural and Linguistic Strengths." *English Education* 42 (3): 249-63.

In a Head Start classroom, Souto-Manning examines the role of classroom discourse analysis in helping to change a teacher's perceptions of English language learners from students who need "fixing" to experts from whom teachers may learn, validating minoritized students' cultural and linguistic practices in curriculum and teaching.

Resources (*continues*)

Au, W., A. Brown, and D. Calderón, D. 2016. *Reclaiming the Multicultural Roots of U.S. Curriculum: Communities of Color and Official Knowledge in Education*. New York: Teachers College Press.

The authors explain how children and youth from minoritized backgrounds are given the message that they don't belong when they don't see themselves in the curriculum being taught. And when their images do appear, they are often positioned in problematic ways.

Emdin, C. 2016. *For White Folks Who Teach in the Hood . . . And the Rest of Y'all Too: Reality Pedagogy and Urban Education*. Boston, MA: Beacon Press.

Emdin documents how the lack of engagement by youth of color changed when hip-hop tenets were employed to guide the design and implementation of learning opportunities. Reflecting on his own experience of being rendered invisible and feeling undervalued in urban classrooms, Emdin highlights the need to embrace and respect each student's culture, repositioning them as experts, to foster learning.

Souto-Manning, M., and J. Martell. 2016. *Reading, Writing, and Talk: Inclusive Teaching Strategies for Diverse Learners*, K–2. New York: Teachers College Press.

The authors document the motivation, investment, and academic growth (even by traditional measures of literacy achievement) of young children (kindergarten–second grade) when their linguistic practices are honored and their families' cultural practices are positioned centrally in curriculum and teaching.

SECTION 3

BUT THAT

Strategies, Tools, and Practices for Culturally Relevant Teaching

CARMEN LUGO LLERENA, JESSICA MARTELL, ABIGAIL SALAS MAGUIRE, AND ALICIA ARCE-BOARDMAN

In Section 1, you read about classroom practices that fail to honor students' cultures and funds of knowledge, and in Section 2, Mariana explored what research says about the impact of culturally relevant practices on student achievement. In this section, we explain how we—Carmen, Alicia, Abigail, and Jessica—began engaging in culturally relevant teaching and share some of the strategies, tools, and approaches we employed. Each of us teaches in New York public elementary schools, yet each of our classrooms is different. Despite these differences, we share a common commitment to culturally relevant teaching and the belief that every one of our students is entitled to see the diversities of their community and the world reflected in our classrooms.

A Mindset for Culturally Relevant Teaching

You've decided to engage in culturally relevant teaching, but you're probably wondering what that will look like in your classroom. If you're like us, you want some clarity. You want strategies. You want tools. But before identifying strategies and tools, it's important to develop mindsets that allow you to do the work.

To develop a culturally relevant teaching mindset, it is essential to recognize the infinite capacity of children, or the brilliance of Black and Brown children, as Lisa Delpit (2012) wrote in her book *Multiplication Is for White People: Raising Expectations for Other People's Children.*

Read about Gloria Ladson-Billings' research into teacher mindsets in Section 2, page 30.

As a group of teachers committed to this mindset, we worked to articulate a set of principles that guide our teaching. We reflected on our own experiences as students, our professional experiences and learning, and our dedication to our students. We arrived at five key commitments we have embraced. In our teaching, we strive to:

1. recognize the wealth of knowledge and resources that each family and community has, and help students develop multicultural competence, becoming knowledgeable about and competent in their own culture(s) and at least one other culture
2. make students' histories and identities a central and integral part of the curriculum
3. see and celebrate what students *can* do instead of focusing on their perceived deficits (as defined by society)
4. invite students to name and question injustices in society
5. critically supplement the curriculum, making it not only rigorous, but also more inclusive and culturally relevant.

In the pages that follow, we share teaching stories and strategies from each of our classrooms and we hope that you will see these commitments reflected in them. We start with Carmen's inclusive kindergarten in New York City, where she invited her students to document family literacies with an inquiry into the origins of names. Then, we go to Alicia's school in Long Island, New York, where she invites us to trouble single stories of Latinxs through artifactual literacies. Next, we go to Jessica's dual language second-grade classroom in New York City, where she uses classroom interviews to invite students to rethink ability and disability. In Abigail's fourth-grade classroom, also in New York City, we see a teacher engage her students by elevating the *story* in hi*story* with a powerful read-aloud. We conclude with a cross-grade collaboration between Jessica's and Abigail's students, who engage in story acting (what some call *teatro*), to invite their students to rethink Columbus Day.

What's in a Name?

Welcome to Carmen's kindergarten classroom in a New York City public school! Carmen has been teaching for over fifteen years. Her school, located on the Upper West Side of Manhattan, predominantly serves children of color. Approximately 55 percent of students are Latinx, 25 percent are Black, 70 percent qualify for free or reduced lunch, 15 percent are labeled "English language learners," and 30 percent have individualized educational plans (IEPs). Carmen currently teaches in an Integrated Co-Teaching classroom, which is mindfully structured to meet the needs of four autistic children and eight to twelve neurotypical children. Previously, she taught in a dual language program for eight years.

First Things First: Learn to Pronounce Students' Names

Like you, at the beginning of each school year, Carmen is presented with a list of children's names—her first introduction to the students she will be entrusted to care for, teach, and nurture toward their full potential. Each year, as she reads the list, she looks for children she might know, perhaps siblings or relatives of former students. She wonders about the children these names represent. Who are they? Where do they live? What are their interests, their dislikes? What resources are available to them? And most importantly, how does she pronounce each name?

Mispronouncing students' names, albeit unintentionally, may have lasting effects. In "Teachers, Please Learn Our Names! Racial Microaggressions and the K–12 Classroom," Kohli and Solórzano (2012) argue that "while the racial undertones to the mispronouncing of names in schools are often understated, when analyzed within a context of historical and current day racism, these incidents are racial microaggressions—subtle daily insults that, as a form of racism, support a racial and cultural hierarchy of minority inferiority" (443). When teachers mispronounce students' names, they may foster the notion that students' cultures and identities are not valued, and the students are often left feeling ridiculed or embarrassed, believing their names are troublesome and wishing they were different. Kohli and Solórzano do not suggest that teachers must pronounce their students' names perfectly, but rather that they make a conscious effort to do so. They also stress the importance of shifting the burden from students and their "difficult" names to teachers and their "inability or unwillingness to pronounce students' names" (443) due to lack of exposure and/or articulation challenges.

At the core of "My Name, My Identity," a nationwide campaign spearheaded by the Santa Clara County Office of Education, is the understanding that "by pronouncing students' names correctly, you can foster a sense of belonging and build positive relationships in the classroom, which are crucial for healthy social, psychological, and educational outcomes." The goal of the campaign is to have school community members pledge to "learn about each other's stories, our unique names, and their proper pronunciations."

Carmen has taken that pledge and is committed to pronouncing her students' names in the manner in which their families do. This simple act conveys to the children and their families that they are welcome in her classroom and that their identities will be honored. However, this has not always been part of her practice, and she has not always been aware of the repercussions of not doing so.

Read more about how failing to identify, leverage, and sustain children's rich cultural practices disadvantages them in school in Section 2, beginning on page 20.

Early in her teaching career, Carmen had an Afro-Latinx student in her kindergarten class who appeared to be challenged with following directions. A couple of weeks into the school year, she decided to share her observations with his mother. She began with "I have noticed that Josiah [She pronounced it Hōsēa, using Spanish conventions] . . ." His slightly annoyed mother interrupted with "Do you mean Josiah (Jōh-sy-uh)? He's always saying, 'Mommy, my teacher doesn't know my name.'" The next day Carmen apologized to Josiah for mispronouncing his name. He smiled and said, "Finally, you know my name!" She learned that Josiah, when referred to as Josiah, followed directions quite nicely. He felt present and validated. He belonged. After all, children's names are the essence of their identity.

Tap into Family Literacies: An Inquiry into the History of Names

After teaching for a few years, Carmen realized that while correctly pronouncing students' names was a meaningful way to honor their identities, she could delve deeper with names and further nurture students' cultural competence. After all, no two Marías, Ryans, or Lins are the same. Each child's name has a meaningful and unique story that reflects a family's traditions, heritage, and culture. Carmen wondered about these stories and if her students knew why their particular names were chosen for them.

Naming a child can be an emotional, painstaking process. Expecting parents may thoughtfully consider a child's gender, ethnicity, heritage, and religion to select a name that is just right. Names may come from pop culture, family members, historic events, or suggestions from others. Our charge as teachers is to know what is unique and special about each child we teach; and inquiring about the meaning and stories of their names is a good place to start—especially as students are learning to read and write their names.

Carmen began the name inquiry by explaining to the children she taught and their families that the class was going to write a name book. They would be conducting family interviews to learn about the history of their names. Carmen invited her students' families to collaborate in the inquiry by providing a simple narrative about how and why their child's name was chosen. She was particularly mindful of how she extended the invitation to each family. She considered factors that typically impede families from receiving communications from the school community. She asked herself questions such as:

Does the family have Internet access? Do they access the Internet on a regular basis?

Although some families prefer emails, for others email creates an unnecessary obstacle. Carmen adjusted her ways of reaching out so that families' preferences were honored.

Do written notices actually make it home or are they lost along the way?

Instead of blaming family members for not sending information back, Carmen re-sent the notices and sought ways to let families know to look out for them. She asked older siblings to alert parents to check backpacks. She also sent parents text messages and made phone calls to inform them that an important notice was on its way.

Is there a language barrier? Can caregivers read and write?

Whenever there was a language barrier, Carmen found translators in the school or community. For example, for one child, the form went home in Arabic. When family members could not read and/or write, Carmen spoke with them on the phone or in person.

Are families overwhelmed with the notion of one more thing on the to-do list?

Carmen asked families how she could help to ensure their participation, explaining how fundamental their involvement was in their child's learning. She offered to scribe over the phone or in person at dismissal. This was especially helpful to parents with younger children, because they could still keep an eye on the little ones as they provided the information needed.

Although it's easy to create excuses for not engaging with children's families, teachers who are committed to culturally relevant teaching must identify resources that enhance access, and to do so, flexibility is key. Be prepared to send plenty of kind reminders and thank-you notes.

Inquiry Invitation: No Name Is the Same

Dear Families,

Our class is excited to announce that we will be conducting an inquiry into the history of each of our names. After all, no name is the same; each one of our names has a unique story behind it. We kindly ask for your help because you are the primary source of knowledge on this topic. Please write a short narrative or a few sentences describing how your child's name was selected. Who suggested or chose the name? Why was it selected? When was it selected? What does it mean?

Thank you for your help with this special project. Please let us know if you have any questions. The history of each of our names will be featured in a class book, which we are looking forward to sharing with all of you in the near future.

In a powerful collaboration with families, the inquiry resulted in a class book of name stories, *No Name is The Same*, a text that was meaningful to the children because it portrayed their unique identities. The inquiry helped children see their family members as knowledgeable experts, and it made space for family literacies to become a central part of curriculum and teaching. When the book was shared for the first time, the children beamed with pride as their stories were read. They made important connections such as being named after an ancestor or a Biblical figure.

Collaborative bookmaking can be a culturally relevant practice when it:

- honors students' lives by permanently capturing their stories, interests, and ideas
- showcases the wealth of difference in the community—look at all of us together!
- allows students to revisit their stories and ideas again and again
- teaches students the power of literacy.

The students each received a copy of *No Name Is the Same* to take home, and Carmen kept a copy of the popular book for her classroom library and another for shared reading. The format of this version was modeled after one developed by preservice teachers and children working with Susi Long, a professor of Early Childhood Education at the University of South Carolina. During a literacy methods course, Susi wanted her students to understand the importance of children's names and family stories as foundational to valuing each other as members of a beautifully diverse world *and* to literacy learning. To do so, the preservice teachers and their child partners researched the children's name stories and developed a predictable text to open and close each page. Using the same predictable pattern, Carmen found that the repetition made reading the book accessible—immediately readable, allowing students to develop what Marie Clay (2000) called "concepts about print." Through repeated readings and with Carmen's guidance, students learned concepts such as print awareness, one-to-one correspondence, directionality, parts of a book, and so on, from a meaningful and culturally relevant text they had created. Figure 3.1 shows a sample page from the book:

To learn more about how culturally relevant texts support literacy learning

See Section 2, page 47.

Nevaeh Aminah Caines

Nevaeh is my name,
No Nevaeh is the same.
Read along to find out
What my name is all about.

My name is Nevaeh. My mommy
said I was a miracle. I am from
heaven. My first name is Heaven
spelled backwards.

Aminah is my middle name. It is
the same name as my daddy's
aunt.

I love my name story!

I Love my Nas ore

My name story
Has come to an end
Turn the page
And meet my friend!

Figure 3.1 Sample Page from the Class Book of Names

No Name Is the Same is only one of many possible inquiries to showcase your students' identities and tap into their families' funds of knowledge, and it's not just an appropriate engagement for young children. Older students can collaborate to explore their identities in similar ways. Other possible inquiries include:

On My Way to School

The Day I Was Born

I Am From . . .

Favorite Places in Our Neighborhood

When I Grow Up I'll Be . . .

Outside My Window I Hear . . .

Our Favorite Family Traditions.

Rethinking Hispanic Heritage Month

Alicia, a Latinx woman whose parents emigrated from Paraguay and Mexico, has taught for almost ten years in a suburban school in New

York State. The school where she teaches serves mostly children of color: 60 percent of the families are Latinx, and almost 40 percent are Black. Thirty percent have been labeled "English Language Learners," and 70 percent qualify for free and/or reduced lunch according to New York State records.

As we explained in Section 1, when she became a teacher, Alicia was committed to making Latinx students' histories and identities integral to both her teaching and the life of the school where she taught. In her new school, she immediately joined the group of teachers who organized celebrations for Hispanic Heritage Month. She knew the solution was not to study the heritage of Latinx students in one month, but this was a way for one teacher to get started recognizing whose histories were visible and invisible in the school where she taught.

Although the committee invested a lot of time in planning the celebrations for Hispanic Heritage Month, as happens in a lot of schools, they were superficial and often reinforced cultural stereotypes. Everyone enjoyed the music, the food, and the celebration of Spanish-speaking countries during this time, but Alicia knew that this wasn't enough. The students, teachers, and community members were not learning about the rich diversity of Latinx culture by merely eating the food, waving a flag, and dancing.

Respectfully but critically, Alicia invited her colleagues to search for ways to make these celebrations more authentic, meaningful, and purposeful. She wanted them to become more central to curriculum and teaching—influencing what went on in classrooms and becoming part of the school's academics.

Artifactual Literacy: Every Object Has a Story

During a visit to *El Museo del Barrio* in East Harlem, New York City, Alicia was inspired by an exhibit that featured artifacts donated by the East Harlem community—kitchen items, posters, paintings, dishes, and so many others. Beautifully authentic, the display was rich with culture and embodied the diverse families in East Harlem. The exhibit communicated the central tenet of artifactual literacy, that *every object tells a story* (Pahl and Rowsell 2010). The artifacts reminded Alicia of her family and the meaningful objects that were part of her life and the stories they told. She thought about the diverse families in her school and wondered if an exhibit like this could be used to celebrate Latinx heritage in ways that were both meaningful and relatable.

Alicia brought the idea of creating an artifact museum back to her school. Not everyone was in favor of the idea at first, preferring to celebrate Hispanic Heritage Month the way they always had. But when parents were invited to weigh in and choose between a having a food

Create an Artifact Museum to Explore Culture

- Consider sharing some of your own artifacts and their stories with your students and model the thinking behind why you selected them. Alicia brought in a doll from her childhood and shared stories of her mother and grandmother.

- Encourage students to talk to their families about which artifacts they will contribute to the museum. They might ask, "What objects help tell the story of who we are?"

- Make a space to display the artifacts, and let your students help you decide how to organize the display. Each child might have his or her own display, or you might group the artifacts by type, function, time period, country of origin, or any other grouping that makes sense based on what you have.

- Invite people to visit the museum and let students be tour guides, explaining the significance of different objects.

- Consider having students write a short explanation of each artifact that becomes part of the display. Or, if you're feeling particularly ambitious, you might have students write a script and record an audio guide like the ones found in other museums.

- Make curricular connections wherever you see them. Artifacts might prompt further research and writing. Or students might serve as curators of the collection, recording, organizing and graphing the contents of the museum.

celebration (as in years past) or creating a home-based museum of arti-facts, they responded with a resounding *yes* to the museum.

As students began bringing in their artifacts to display, the museum filled with coffee cups, plates, pictures, statues, flags, key chains—but more importantly, it filled with stories. As stu-dents shared those stories, they brought meaning to the objects and the role each one played in their families within and across generations. The objects and the stories were windows into the

See Section 2 to learn more about the importance of understanding the cultural practices in students' homes and communities.

many cultural practices of the community. They were both seamlessly incorporated into the curriculum: first, as students engaged in primary source research, taking notes and learning from family members, and then, later, as students engaged in both descriptive and narrative writing about the objects.

The enthusiasm for the artifact museum was contagious, and the museum eventually grew so much that it spilled out into the hallways of the school. Students and staff members who passed by the displays regularly on their way to gym or lunch were inspired to add their own artifacts. What began as a celebration of Hispanic Heritage Month grew into an even bigger celebration of the diversity of the school. Because of the museum, students saw diversities within Latinxs—an often stereotyped and essentialized cultural group.

Video: A Power Tool for Developing Cross-Cultural Understandings

The following year, the task was to (re)create a celebration that was equally inspiring and authentic. Alicia knew that the stories of the stu-dents and their families were important and still needed to be told, especially considering the current political climate around the topic of immigration. This time, to make even stronger connections to the academic curriculum, she used the book *¡Sí! Somos Latinos (Yes! We Are Latinos)* by Alma Flor Ada and F. Isabel Campoy as a mentor text.

Ada's book is a collection of narratives representing young Latinxs of diverse backgrounds. After reading and discussing the book, Alicia's students had a better grasp of how stories help them understand people's cultural practices and experiences, illustrating diversities within cultural groups. Soon after, they embarked on an oral history project to capture the unique stories of all Latinx students and staff members in the school. Videorecording, students interviewed their peers and teachers, who talked about their (or their families') transitions to the United States from their home countries. The interviews were compiled into a video created by the English as a new language (ENL) teacher (Perez 2015).

As a celebration, the entire school community, including students' families, settled into the auditorium on a Friday morning in October. Once the lights were turned off, students walked on stage and recited excerpts from *¡Sí! Somos Latinos (Yes! We Are Latinos)*, making clear the rich diversity of Latinx culture. Then the music started, and the audience sat in awe as the stories of students and staff members were brought to life on the large screen through an amazing digital compilation of student interviews, narratives, and music.

The video had a tremendous impact. The stories captured by the students challenged everyone in attendance to learn more about Latinx cultures and urged them not to oversimplify a very diverse group of people with rich histories and historical practices.

> Video is a simple but powerful tool for culturally relevant teaching. Why? Because it forces students to *see* and *hear* people and to consider them in ways that statistics and even written words obscure. Video data add an important, affective dimension to any research. Consider all the ways you might use video or videoconferencing tools to enhance your curriculum and put your students in touch with the faces, voices, stories and knowledge of people of multiple backgrounds and cultures.

Learning from Classroom Interviews

Jessica—a New York City public school teacher for over twenty years—teaches in the East Harlem community where she's lived her entire life. Her family is from Puerto Rico. The school where she teaches serves mostly children of color: 35 percent of the families are Latinx and close to 30 percent are Black. One hundred percent qualify for free or reduced lunch. Twenty percent have IEPs.

In her second-grade classroom, Jessica works to position her students centrally in the curriculum. She uses classroom interviews to provide mirrors and windows into each other's lives, celebrating what individuals can do instead of focusing on their perceived deficits (as defined by society). By teaching her students to be thoughtful and curious interviewers, Jessica shows them *how* to learn from and about multiple perspectives, a skill she hopes will help them be culturally sensitive and aware long after they leave her classroom.

Funds of Knowledge: Who Do We Have Here?

Jessica begins every school year with a My Child information sheet. The sheet includes questions about the child's name, address, emergency contact number, and family members' email addresses, but it also asks parents to share additional information, tips, and bits of advice about their children. Questions include the following:

Read the research about the importance of tapping funds of knowledge in Section 2, beginning on page 41.

- What would you like me to know about your child?
- What does your child enjoy doing at home?
- What are your goals for your child this year?
- What do you enjoy doing with your child/children?
- What would your child tell us that you are very good at? Why?

- Would you be interested in sharing your hobbies or interests with the class?
- Would you be willing to teach us about your skill/experience/expertise?

As the sheets are returned, Jessica highlights and makes notes on them to start identifying the "funds of knowledge" and mapping the human resources available in the larger classroom community. To ensure equity of voices, Jessica reaches out to any parent who does not respond in writing. As she notes what each family is willing to contribute to the class, the map serves as a resource she'll tap to enrich, deepen, and expand perspectives in her curriculum and teaching. Jessica begins talking to parents about potential visits almost immediately.

Tapping into Funds of Knowledge

- Consider your curriculum. Do your students' families have expertise or access to places or people that would enhance your content or objectives? For example, Jessica always looks for family members who might work at the city's parks, local businesses, or landmarks because the geography and history of New York City are part of the second-grade curriculum.

- Look for counternarratives. Do your students' families have perspectives to offer that might disrupt preconceptions and stereotypes? For example, Jessica seeks out moms who might work in a field dominated by men, or families who speak languages besides English, or fathers who are primary caretakers.

- Think about your students. Do students' family members have occupations or expertise that match your students' interests and curiosities? Or mandated standards? For example, children who love to race each other on the playground might be fascinated by an older brother who's on the high school track team or a parent who runs marathons.

The families in Jessica's class quickly come to realize that their input in the classroom is valued. They are regarded as teachers, as experts, and as individuals, and they come to understand the value in their own skills, contributions, and stories. Once families see that they are helping shape the curriculum, they almost always add to the list initially offered in the My Child sheet, expanding the available funds of knowledge. As the year progresses, parents frequently request to come in and teach the class. Jessica has had parents ask to share their experience preparing for and running a marathon and to facilitate architectural studies of the local neighborhood (helping her address academic areas such as science and math in meaningful ways). Each time, these visits have direct links to learning standards and enrich the curriculum in situated and culturally relevant ways.

Teaching Students to Interview

Inviting family members to share their expertise is only the beginning. Jessica also knows she has to teach her students *how* to learn from others' knowledge and experiences, so she begins coaching them to construct and ask meaningful questions from the very first classroom interview. As students prepare for each visitor, they're encouraged to research and inquire about the topic of the interview. Then, Jessica works with them to understand the "curriculum" of interviewing:

- Begin by thinking about what you really want to learn from the person being interviewed.
- Ask questions that require some thought, rather than a yes-or-no answer.
- Make sure your questions are related to the person's expertise or experience. If you're interviewing an architect, your questions should be about the interviewee's knowledge of architecture.
- Personal questions are fine, but they should be meaningful. Rather than, "How old are you?" you might ask, "How old were you when you decided you wanted to become an architect?"
- Listen carefully to the responses, and be ready to ask follow-up questions if you have them.

Before a visitor arrives, Jessica and her students generate a list of questions for the interviewee. Their preparation sends an important message to the family members who give them their time: *What you have to offer us is valuable and we've thought a lot about it.* As students conduct their interviews, Jessica carefully observes them and takes notes on what she needs to teach them to become even better at interviewing.

By the end of the year, interviewing becomes central to the classroom and is the main tool through which Jessica's students learn from others and consider different perspectives in all areas of the curriculum. To understand what this tool looks like in action, consider the story of an interview that took place in the very last week of the school year in Jessica's classroom. This story will also expand the conversation about culturally relevant teaching to include seeing and embracing the diversity of differently abled people.

The Story of a Powerful Interview

Nathan's grandmother, Lola, was visiting New York City from Connecticut, and Nathan's classmates had never met her. Nathan's mom, Loysa, asked Jessica if Lola could visit the class, and then she added that Lola would also bring Kava. "Who's Kava?" Jessica asked.

"A dog," Loysa answered.

Kava was a very important member of Nathan's family, and he really wanted his classmates to meet the dog. Lola is legally blind and Kava is her Seeing Eye dog. Jessica was thrilled that Lola wanted to visit, and despite the challenge of scheduling on the last days of school, Jessica asked if the family could visit that Friday afternoon.

As she thought about preparing for the upcoming visit, Jessica realized there was not one book in her classroom that depicted the culture of the blind. Not one! Jessica asked Nathan to explain who Lola and Kava were so the students would have some prior knowledge. For most of them, this would be their first time talking with a blind person. Some of the children had seen Seeing Eye dogs guide their owners, but they'd never been able to get their questions answered. And even though 40 percent of the children in Jessica's class had identified disabilities, they had not had the opportunity to address disabilities through family interviews. This opportunity would allow her students to see and celebrate what individuals with varying abilities can do, from an assets-based perspective, instead of focusing on their deficits.

On the day of the interview, Loysa entered the room first and shared the rules with regards to Kava. The children were to sit calmly and not touch Kava. They could ask questions but needed to wait until Lola was seated and Kava was calm. Nathan would call on the students for questions. Jessica let Lola and Kava into the room. The students sat in silent excitement. Kava quickly lay at Lola's feet. Lola began her story.

Jessica noticed the students were calmer than usual. They listened and smiled to Lola's explanation of how she and Kava met. They waited patiently for a turn to ask their questions. Jessica could see that their yearlong experiences as interviewers allowed them to ask thoughtful questions such as:

Are people born blind or can they become blind?

Many children did not know that one could become blind. Lola lost her vision in her fifties.

What does "legally blind" mean?

This was a question even the adults in the room wanted to know.

Was Kava born a Seeing Eye dog?

This question led to an inquiry on which breeds can be trained to become Seeing Eye dogs.

What training did Kava receive to become a Seeing Eye dog?

She trained for many months before becoming a guide dog.

How were you (Lola) and Kava matched?

They were assigned to work together. Some matches don't work.

After the interview was over and Lola removed Kava's guide, the students were allowed to touch Kava. Although a couple of students jumped at the chance to touch Kava, most gathered around Lola and continued asking her questions. The school bell rang to end the day, but the questions continued. They continued all the way to the dismissal yard.

Kava and Lola provided a window into the lives of the blind for Jessica's students. Not only did Lola answer questions, but she and Kava humanized disabilities by allowing students to see through windows into her culture, not judgmentally, but with genuine interest in the diversities inherent to the human family.

Jessica's students learned that their curiosities and questions can lead to great discoveries. Not only did they learn the art of constructing and asking meaningful questions, but they used their curiosities to learn from other people's experiences and understand multiple perspectives, not just a single viewpoint. This is what makes interviewing a powerful tool for culturally relevant teaching.

Elevating the *Story* in History

Abigail has been a teacher in New York City public schools for twelve years. She currently teaches fourth grade in a dual language classroom in a school serving mostly children of color (55 percent Latinx, 24 percent Black), where 70 percent of the children receive free or reduced-price lunch.

As a child, Abigail thought she hated history. It was the dates—she just couldn't remember the dates. She could tell you about Martin Luther King's "I Have a Dream" speech and how Emiliano Zapata gathered his group of Zapatistas as part of the Mexican Revolution. But if you asked her when, she couldn't tell you. She couldn't tell her teachers. And so she did not do well in social studies and thought that she hated history.

When Abigail started teaching, teaching history was her biggest struggle. No matter how much she tried to explain why Europeans came to the "New World" (a staple of the fourth-grade curriculum), no matter how much she tried to get her students to question why explorers from Italy, France, England, Portugal, and Spain wanted to explore and conquer, they still didn't really care. How was she supposed to make history interesting to her students? How could she help them see the way their culture is shaped by history and question whose stories are told—especially a problematic history that colonized populations to which her students' families and communities belonged? In a word, how could she make it *relevant*? She knew that rather than focus on dates, she had to focus on the what-ifs, hows, and whys.

Read-Aloud as a Tool to Trouble the Single Story

As Columbus Day was approaching one year, Abigail came across a picture book titled *Encounter*, written by Jane Yolen and illustrated by David Shannon. The illustrations in the book are dark and powerful, and the story is hard to forget. A work of historical fiction, *Encounter* is the story of Christopher Columbus' arrival in the "New World"—specifically San Salvador—told from the perspective of a Taíno child. The child is suspicious of Columbus and tries to warn his people that Columbus has more devious plans than just exploring.

Because the book was available in both English and Spanish, Abigail thought it would be a helpful read-aloud in her dual language classroom. Although *Encounter* introduces problematic ideas, such as the fact that there are no more Taínos today, Abigail decided she would invite her students to consider a different perspective on Columbus' arrival from the widely popularized (and highly problematic) one in their social studies textbook.

The read-aloud turned out to be a powerful engagement for her fourth-grade students, so for several years, the Friday before Columbus Day, Abigail would engage in a critical reading of *Encounter*. Her students were always shocked at the staggering number of Taínos who died due to sickness after Columbus' arrival. They were always left saddened to hear that Columbus and his crew kidnapped many and

To be critically conscious is to acknowledge, understand, and trouble how the culture of power silences and marginalizes certain perspectives.

See Section 2, page 44.

enslaved indigenous peoples. They were curious, confused, and angry, but most importantly, they began to ask significant questions:

- *How could the Taínos let this happen?*
- *Why didn't they listen to the boy when he said that Christopher Columbus looked dangerous?*
- *Is it really true that the Taínos are all dead?*

What a book like *Encounter* offers students is a way to understand history through *story*. Abigail's fourth graders related to this child the adults ignored, and history came alive for them. History, of course, is not just dates and events. History *happened* to, with, and through people. Sharing books that tell stories of people is one very simple, profound way to engage students in learning about history. And for teachers committed to culturally relevant practices, it's critically important that they share both narrative and informational texts (many of which are quite compelling as well) that offer students multiple perspectives on the same history.

Questions to Help You Think About Historical Fiction

- Who is narrating the story?
- What role does the narrator play in the historical event?
- What other characters speak?
- Whose voices are not heard?
- In a picture book, how do the illustrations contribute to the story?
- Does the story "trouble" or challenge the widely accepted version of history?
- What questions does this story raise for you? What else do you want to know?

Resources for Finding Culturally Relevant Texts

As you consider ways to bring culturally relevant practices to your curriculum, think about how you might go beyond your content-specific textbooks and find culturally relevant trade literature to share with students. Here are some websites that offer book lists to help get you started. Each of these organizations is committed to helping teachers find books that truly represent the diversity of children:

- http://weneeddiversebooks.org
- https://ccbc.education.wisc.edu/books/bibBio.asp
- www.colorincolorado.org/books-authors
- www.lacasaazulbookstore.com
- www.tolerance.org.

Experiencing Multiple Perspectives Through Story Acting

For a time, Abigail and Jessica taught in the same school. Columbus Day provided the context for a powerful collaboration between their two classes. As the holiday was approaching, Jessica's second-grade students were wondering about the day off from school. "Another holiday?" one asked. Although Columbus' role in the colonization of the Americas was not in the second-grade curriculum, Jessica's students demanded answers regarding the holiday. "What is so important about Columbus that he gets a holiday?"

Jessica didn't have the time to teach her students about Columbus' voyage and conquests, and she really didn't *want* to teach about the holiday and what it meant. Although she strongly believed in one perspective of the Columbus story, Jessica had never taught that perspective because she had seen teaching as neutral, as apolitical. She had never wanted her students to know what she thought because she knows how much a teacher can influence what students think and believe. Year after year she avoided teaching about the subject, but this year was different.

Based on the work of the renowned Brazilian theater director Augusto Boal, and his *Theater of the Oppressed* (1979), story acting is a method that aims to transform spectators into active actors in a theatrical experience. In the classroom, story acting can be a tool to help students develop empathy and expand their understandings. Rather than developing a script and then performing, with story acting participants take action as they would in real life, but within the context of a dramatized situation. See also page 77.

This year, in response to her students' demands, Jessica decided to engage them in rethinking Columbus Day. Most of them knew something of the "sanctioned" story of Columbus, but she wanted them to better understand the perspective of the indigenous peoples—or at least to empathize with them. What it means to be conquered—to have your home taken over by strangers—can be difficult for children to grasp because it just seems so far from anything most of them have experienced. After lots of reflection, Jessica decided to use a form of story acting to help her students understand the concept and begin questioning the single story of Columbus.

With an idea for a cross-grade collaboration, Jessica approached Abigail and together they made a plan for Abigail's fourth-grade students to enact a "conquering" of Jessica's classroom—using the furniture and materials as if they were their own—while the second graders were unaware and away in the gym. When Jessica's students returned, both the teachers and the student "conquerors" would engage in story acting for a few minutes.

On the day of the dramatization, the fourth graders arrived in Jessica's room soon after the second-grade students had left for the gym, so they had almost an hour to settle in and get used to the space before the story acting began. As Jessica walked her students back to the classroom, she gave them no clue about what was about to happen. She really wanted them to experience whatever natural reactions and emotions they would have to the experience, and her first job as a facilitator was to be a part of the acting. When they arrived at her door, Jessica gave them routine directions, "OK, second graders, when you enter the classroom, please put your writing notebooks on the tables and let's meet in the meeting area." As they entered the classroom, many of them froze at the unexpected sight of the older children spread across the room.

For several minutes, Abigail, her fourth graders, and Jessica engaged in story acting in a drama about a classroom that had been "discovered and claimed." From their actions, the fourth grade students clearly felt powerful, but Jessica's students' reactions were markedly different. Some reacted with anger, others with fear and confusion. Several were complacent and willing to share. And only one student smiled, as he waved to his sister in Abigail's class.

When Abigail and Jessica decided to end the role-playing, the two classes came together to reflect on what had happened and share what they were thinking and feeling as the drama unfolded. Reflection and dialogue are key to the development of understanding and empathy through story acting. Abigail's students discussed how they enjoyed the conquest and felt powerful, while Jessica's students shared that they were scared and some even "felt like crying." Connections were immediately made to Columbus, his conquistadores, and the indigenous peoples of the "new found land," and students began to question the single story they'd always heard about Columbus "discovering" America:

- *Did Columbus create slavery?*
- *How can people celebrate Columbus Day?*
- *Why couldn't the two groups just share?*
- *How can anyone find something that wasn't lost?*

Jessica and Abigail never shared their own views on Columbus that day. They didn't need to. They positioned themselves as actors. They embodied history. They experienced emotions alongside their students (Jessica explained that she felt like crying). The students learned through doing, and they shared and questioned their own perspectives and the perspectives of their peers.

Tips for Using Story Acting in the Classroom

- The setting and plot for the story may come from history or from current events, or it may be an imagined story that helps students understand something about the human condition (for example, what it means to be conquered).

- In the example we shared, Jessica and Abigail chose not to reveal the story to the second graders beforehand. Often actors are well aware of the story, and revelations come as they improvise and react to the drama as it unfolds. In this case, Abigail's fourth graders were aware that they were acting as Christopher Columbus and his crew.

- Guidelines and expectations have to be established. There has to be respect and rapport among the community of learners. Jessica and Abigail co-created a safe space for students to take risks and co-construct these stories.

- It is necessary to blur the roles of teacher and learner. Jessica and Abigail were learning right along with their students, especially during the time of reflection.

- Take the time to reflect. Students will have different feelings, questions, and perspectives. This reflection time is when the students will learn the most from each other.

Whether it's in a cross-grade collaboration such as this, or in a single classroom, whether students are enacting a drama about history or one about yesterday's news story, story acting is a culturally relevant teaching tool because it helps students develop empathy while accessing and understanding multiple perspectives.

Culturally Relevant Teaching Is Essential, Now More Than Ever

We are a group of teachers committed to culturally relevant teaching. We hope the examples we shared affirm that when we teach students in ways that allow them to see themselves in the curriculum, we deem their histories and identities powerful. But please remember, culturally relevant teaching is much bigger than any single engagement, project, or activity. Relevance needs to wrap around everything that happens in a classroom. Whether in kindergarten, second, or fourth grade, we see our students as capable learners, and we foster respect and high expectations. When we are constrained by the curriculum guide adopted by the schools where we teach, we critically supplement the curriculum, making it more inclusive and culturally relevant.

As we get to know the children we teach and who they are within the context of their families and communities, we are better able to support their learning—and create multiple opportunities for them to learn and develop mastery. Regardless of the process, we each recognize that culturally relevant teaching addresses learning standards. In fact, it often requires going *beyond* mandated learning standards. It is not fluff. It is not optional. It is foundational. It is rigorous. Culturally relevant teaching is essential.

As you engage in this kind of teaching, always remember that culturally *ir*relevant teaching continues to promote inequities, to tell students of color and students multiply minoritized by schools and society that they don't matter . . . that their lives don't matter. As teachers, we have the responsibility to take a visible stand and show students that their lives *do* matter . . . in teaching, in learning, and in society.

Ready? Now, let's get started!

AFTERWORD
Nell K. Duke

In 1943 a psychologist named Abraham Maslow developed a theory of motivation that included a hierarchy of human needs. Most basic in the hierarchy are physiological needs, such as the needs for food, water, and sleep. Next above those is the need for safety and security. Just above that are what Maslow called the "love needs." He argued that these needs include a need not only for affection but also for belongingness. A person "will hunger for affectionate relations with people in general, namely, for a place in his group, and he will strive with great intensity to achieve this goal" (Maslow 1943, 381). When the materials and practices we use in the classroom lead children to feel that they don't belong, that they don't have a place in the group, we are, in Maslow's terms, undermining a fundamental human need.

The next category in Maslow's hierarchy includes "esteem needs." Among other things, Maslow contends "we have what we may call the desire for reputation or prestige (defining it as respect or esteem from other people), recognition, attention, importance or appreciation" (381–82). In this domain, it is not enough to feel simply tolerated or even included, but to feel that you, and by extension the cultural group(s) with which you identify, are valued and appreciated. To foster this feeling in children sets a still higher bar for the materials and practices we enact in the classroom.

Although Maslow put forth these ideas over seventy years ago, and they have received a great deal of attention and evolved considerably since that time, their implications for classrooms have yet to be fully realized. Mariana Souto-Manning, Carmen Lugo Llerena, Jessica Martell, Abigail Salas Maguire, and Alicia Arce-Boardman have made an important contribution to helping us understand ways in which we can foster belongingness and esteem through the curricular and pedagogical choices that we make. Culturally relevant teaching is an essential tool toward that end.

Both from my personal experience and from many conversations with teachers, I realize that the move toward more culturally relevant teaching can feel overwhelming. The portraits of powerfully responsive teaching included in this book may feel intimidating as well as inspiring. A move toward culturally relevant teaching, however, is a process—one that can continue throughout a career. I encourage you to take this work in steps, and particularly to take the most important step: the first one. Perhaps your first step is a critical examination of the books you read aloud to children or perhaps it's shifting the way you begin the year or perhaps it's endeavoring to learn more about your students' families. This book has provided a wealth of guidance on these and many more steps we can take to meeting all of our children's needs.

REFERENCES

Ada, A. F., and F. Isabel Campoy 2013. *Yes! We Are Latinos: Poems and Prose About the Latino Experience.* Illustrated by David Diaz. Watertown, MA: Charlesbridge.

———. 2014. *¡Sí! Somos Latinos.* Illustrated by David Diaz. Doral, FL: Santillana.

Adichie, C. "Chimamanda Adichie: The Danger of a Single Story." Filmed July 2009. TED video, 18:49. www.ted.com/talks/chimamanda_adichie_the_danger_of_a_single_story.html.

Ahmed, F., and F. Narcy-Combes. 2011. "An Analysis of Textbooks from a Cultural Point of View." *TESOL Journal* 5: 21–37.

Amanti, C. 2005. "Beyond a Beads and Feathers Approach." In *Funds of Knowledge: Theorizing Practices in Households, Communities, and Classrooms,* edited by N. González, L. C. Moll, and C. Amanti, 131–41. Mahwah, NJ: Lawrence Erlbaum Associates.

Aronson, B., and J. Laughter. 2016. "The Theory and Practice of Culturally Relevant Education: A Synthesis of Research Across Content Areas." *Review of Educational Research* 86(1): 163–206.

Au, K. 1980. "Participation Structures in a Reading Lesson with Hawaiian Children: Analysis of a Culturally Appropriate Instructional Event." *Anthropology & Education Quarterly* 11(2): 91–115.

Au, W., ed. 2014. *Rethinking Multicultural Education: Teaching for Racial and Culture Justice* 2nd ed. Milwaukee, WI: Rethinking Schools.

Au, W., A. Brown, and D. Calderón. 2016. *Reclaiming the Multicultural Roots of U.S. Curriculum: Communities of Color and Official Knowledge in Education.* New York: Teachers College Press.

Banks, J. A. 2016. "Series Foreword." In *Reclaiming the Multicultural Roots of U.S. Curriculum: Communities of Color and Official Knowledge in Education,* edited by W. Au, A. Brown, and D. Calderón, 11–15. New York: Teachers College Press.

Bell, Y., and T. Clark. 1998. "Culturally Relevant Reading Material as Related to Comprehension and Recall in African American Children." *Journal of Black Psychology* 24(4): 455–75.

Bishop, R. S. 1990. "Mirrors, Windows, and Sliding Glass Doors." *Perspectives* 6(3): ix–xi.

———. 2015. "Mirrors, Windows, and Sliding Doors." *Reading Rockets.org.* www.youtube.com/watch?v=_AAu58SNSyc.

Boal, A. 1979. *Theater of the Oppressed.* New York: Theater Communications Group.

Brown, A., and W. Au. 2014. "Race, Memory, and Master Narratives: A Critical Essay on U.S. Curriculum History." *Curriculum Inquiry* 44(3): 358–89.

Bui, Y. N., and Y. M. Fagan. 2013. "The Effects of an Integrated Reading Comprehension Strategy: A Culturally Responsive Teaching Approach for Fifth-Grade Students' Reading Comprehension." *Preventing School Failure* 57: 59–69.

Cahnmann, M. S., and J. T. Remillard. 2002. "What Counts and How: Mathematics Teaching in Culturally, Linguistically, and Socioeconomically Diverse Urban Settings." *The Urban Review* 34(3): 179–204.

Carter, R., and A. L. Goodwin. 1994. "Racial Identity and Education." *Review of Research in Education* 20: 291–336.

Cayton, A., E. Perry, L. Reed, and A. Winker. 2007. *America: Pathways to the Present—Modern American History.* Boston, MA: Prentice Hall.

Clay, M. 2000. *Concepts About Print.* Portsmouth, NH: Heinemann.

Commonwealth of Australia. 2009. *Belonging, Being & Becoming: The Early Years Learning Framework for Australia.* https://docs.education.gov.au/system/files/doc /other/belonging_being_and_becoming_the_early_years_learning_framework_for _australia.pdf.

Coughran, M. J. 2012. "Enacting Culturally Relevant Pedagogy: Going Beyond Heroes and Holidays Curriculum." Master's thesis, Mills College, Oakland, CA. Available from Proquest Dissertations and Theses Database. UMI No. 1510828. http://pqdtopen.proquest.com/doc/1018720319.html?FMT=AI.

Delpit, L. 1988. "The Silenced Dialogue: Power and Pedagogy in Educating Other People's Children." *Harvard Educational Review* 58(3): 280–99.

———. 1995. *Other People's Children: Cultural Conflict in the Classroom.* New York: New Press.

———. 2012. *Multiplication Is for White People: Raising Expectations for Other People's Children.* New York: The New Press.

Educational Research Analysts. 2002. "Worse Than Before: Citizens 249, Education Establishment 0." www.textbookreviews.org/index.html?content=nl_11_02.htm.

Emdin, C. 2016. *For White Folks Who Teach in the Hood . . . and the Rest of Y'all Too: Reality Pedagogy and Urban Education.* Boston, MA: Beacon Press.

Feger, M.-V. 2006. "'I Want to Read': How Culturally Relevant Texts Increase Student Engagement in Reading." *Multicultural Education* 13(3): 18–19. http://files .eric.ed.gov/fulltext/EJ759630.pdf.

Freire, P. 1970. *Pedagogy of the Oppressed.* New York: Continuum.

———. 1998. *Teachers as Cultural Workers: Letters to Those Who Dare Teach.* Boulder, CO: Westview.

Gay, G. 1975. "Organizing and Designing Culturally Pluralistic Curriculum." *Educational Leadership* 33(3): 176–83.

———. 1980. "Ethnic Pluralism in Social Studies Education: Where to from Here?" *Social Education* 44(1): 52–55.

———. 2002. "Preparing for Culturally Responsive Teaching." *Journal of Teacher Education* 53(2): 106–16.

———. 2010. *Culturally Responsive Teaching: Theory, Research, and Practice.* 2nd ed. New York: Teachers College Press.

———. 2013. "Teaching to and Through Cultural Diversity." *Curriculum Inquiry* 43(1): 48–70.

Geber, M., and R. F. A. Dean. 1957. "Gesell Tests on African Children." *Pediatrics* 20: 1061–64.

———. 1958. "Psychomotor Development in African Children: The Effects of Social Class and the Need for Improved Tests." *Bulletin of the World Health Organization* 18: 471–76.

González, N. 2005. "Beyond Culture: The Hybridity of Funds of Knowledge." In *Funds of Knowledge: Theorizing Practices in Households, Communities, and Classrooms*, edited by N. González, L. Moll, and C. Amanti, 29–46. Mahwah, NJ: Lawrence Erlbaum Associates.

González, N., L. Moll, and C. Amanti, eds. 2005. *Funds of Knowledge: Theorizing Practices in Households, Communities, and Classrooms.* Mahwah, NJ: Lawrence Erlbaum Associates.

Goodwin, A. L., R. Cheruvu, and C. Genishi. 2008. "Responding to Multiple Diversities in Early Childhood Education." In *Diversities in Early Childhood Education: Rethinking and Doing*, edited by C. Genishi and A. L. Goodwin, 3–10. New York: Routledge.

Grant, C. A., and C. E. Sleeter. 1996. *After the School Bell Rings.* 2nd ed. Philadelphia, PA: Falmer.

Gutiérrez, K., P. Morales, and D. Martínez. 2009. "Re-Mediating Literacy: Culture, Difference, and Learning for Students from Nondominant Communities." *Review of Research in Education* 33: 212–45.

Gutiérrez, R. 2000. "Advancing African-American, Urban Youth in Mathematics: Unpacking the Success of One Math Department." *American Journal of Education* 109(1): 63–111.

Hanley, M. S., and G. Noblit. 2009. "Cultural Responsiveness, Racial Identity, and Academic Success: A Review of Literature." www.heinz.org/userfiles/library/culture-report_final.pdf.

Heath, S. B. 1983. *Ways with Words: Language, Life, and Work in Communities and Classrooms.* New York: Cambridge University Press.

Hensley, M. 2005. "Empowering Parents of Multicultural Backgrounds." In *Funds of Knowledge: Theorizing Practices in Households, Communities, and Classrooms*, edited by N. González, L. C. Moll, and C. Amanti, 143–51. Mahwah, NJ: Lawrence Erlbaum Associates.

Hilliard III, A. 2009. "What Do We Need to Know Now?" In *Rethinking Multicultural Education*, edited by W. Au, 21–36. Milwaukee, WI: Rethinking Schools Publications.

Hollie, S. 2001. "Acknowledging the Language of African American Students: Instructional Strategies." *English Journal* 90(4): 54–59.

Jiménez, R. 1997. "The Strategic Readings Abilities and Potential of Five Low-Literacy Latina/o Readers in Middle School." *Reading Research Quarterly* 32(3): 224–43.

Jiménez, R., and R. Gertsen. 1999. "Lessons and Dilemmas Derived from the Literacy Instruction of Two Latina/o Teachers." *American Educational Research Journal* 36(2): 265–301.

Kohli, R., and D. G. Solórzano. 2012. "Teachers, Please Learn Our Names! Racial Microaggressions and the K–12 Classroom." *Race Ethnicity and Education* 15(4): 441–62.

Ladson-Billings, G. 1994. *The Dreamkeepers: Successful Teachers of African American Children*. San Francisco, CA: Jossey-Bass.

———. 1995a. "'But That's Just Good Teaching!' The Case for Culturally Relevant Pedagogy." *Theory into Practice* 34(3): 159–65.

———. 1995b. "Toward a Theory of Culturally Relevant Pedagogy." *American Education Research Journal* 32(3): 465–91.

———. 2001. *Crossing Over to Canaan: The Journey of New Teachers in Diverse Classrooms*. San Francisco, CA: Jossey Bass.

———. 2006a. "From Achievement Gap to Education Debt: Understanding Achievement in U.S. Schools." *Educational Researcher* 35(7): 3–12.

———. 2006b. "'Yes, But How Do We Do It?' Practicing Culturally Relevant Pedagogy." In *White Teachers/Diverse Classrooms*, edited by J. Landsman and C. Lewis, 29–41. Herndon, VA: Stylus Publishers.

———. 2009. *The Dreamkeepers: Successful Teachers of African American Children*. 2nd ed. San Francisco, CA: Jossey Bass.

———. "In Focus with Gloria Ladson-Billings." Filmed February 3, 2010. Houston A⁺ Challenge Speaker Series. www.youtube.com/watch?v=fQfg-UqkUzE.

———. "Cultural Competency." Filmed Januaray 22, 2012. Youth Wellness video. www.youtube.com/watch?v=XSE8nxxZN5s.

———. "Getting Serious About Education: Culturally Relevant Teaching for New Century Students." Filmed March 25, 2014. John M. Wozniak Lecture Series. www.youtube.com/watch?v=S5asJrgl4_8.

Lee, C. D. 2007. *Culture, Literacy, and Learning: Taking Bloom in the Midst of the Whirlwind.* New York: Teachers College Press.

Leonardo, Z., and W. N. Grubb. 2014. *Education and Racism: A Primer on Issues and Dilemmas.* New York: Routledge.

Loewen, J. 2007. *Lies My Teacher Told Me: Everything Your American History Textbook Got Wrong.* New York: Touchstone.

Martell, C. 2013. "Race and Histories: Examining Culturally Relevant Teaching in the U.S. History Classroom." *Theory & Research in Social Education* 41: 65–88.

Maslow, A. H. 1943. "A Theory of Human Motivation." *Psychological Review* 50(4): 370–96.

McCarty, T. 2005. *Language, Literacy, and Power in Schooling.* Mahwah, NJ: LEA.

McDermott, R., and H. Varenne. 1995. "Culture as Disability." *Anthropology & Education Quarterly* 26(3): 324–48.

McDiarmit, G., and D. Pratt. 1971. *Teaching Prejudice: A Content Analysis of Social Studies Textbooks Authorized for Use in Ontario.* Ontario, CA: OISE.

Mitescu, E., J. Pedulla, M. Cannady, M. Cochran-Smith, and C. Jong. 2011. "Measuring Practices of Teaching for Social Justice in Elementary Mathematics Classrooms." *Educational Research Quarterly* 34(3): 15–39.

Moll, L. C., C. Amanti, D. Neff, and N. González. 1992. "Funds of Knowledge for Teaching: Using a Qualitative Approach to Connect Homes and Classrooms." *Theory into Practice* 31(2): 132–41.

Moll, L. C., and J. Greenberg. 1990. "Creating Zones of Possibilities: Combining Social Contexts for Instruction." In *Vygotsky and Education*, edited by L. C. Moll, 319–48. Cambridge, UK: Cambridge University Press.

Morrison, K., H. Robbins, and D. Rose. 2008. "Operationalizing Culturally Relevant Pedagogy: A Synthesis of Classroom-Based Research." *Equity & Excellence in Education* 41: 433–52.

National Center for Education Statistics. 2014. "Table 105.30. Enrollment in Elementary, Secondary, and Degree-Granting Postsecondary Institutions, by Level and Control of Institution: Selected years, 1869–70 through fall 2024." http://nces.ed.gov/programs/digest/d14/tables/dt14_105.30.asp.

Ndura, E. 2004. "ESL and Cultural Bias: An Analysis of Elementary Through High School Textbooks in the Western United States of America." *Language, Culture and Curriculum* 17(2): 143–53.

Nieto, S. 2010. *The Light in Their Eyes: Creating Multicultural Learning Communities.* 10th anniversary ed. New York: Teachers College Press.

———. 2013. *Finding Joy in Teaching Students of Diverse Backgrounds: Culturally Responsive and Socially Just Practices in U.S. Classrooms.* Portsmouth, NH: Heinemann.

Pahl, K., and J. Rowsell. 2010. *Artifactual Literacies: Every Object Tells a Story*. New York: Teachers College Press.

Parsons, E. 2005. "From Caring as a Relation to Culturally Relevant Caring: A White Teacher's Bridge to Black Students." *Equity & Excellence in Education* 38(1): 25–34.

Paul, A. W. 2004. *Mañana Iguana*. Illustrated by E. Long. New York, NY: Holiday House.

———. 2007. *Fiesta Fiasco*. Illustrated by E. Long. New York, NY: Holiday House.

———. 2008. *Count on Culebra: Go From 1 to 10 in Spanish*. Illustrated by E. Long. New York, NY: Holiday House.

———. 2009. *Tortuga in Trouble*. Illustrated by E. Long. New York, NY: Holiday House.

Perez, M. 2015. "Somos Latinos." www.youtube.com/watch?v=pECpMSo77Gs.

Reyes, P., J. Scribner, and A. Scribner, eds. 1999. *Lessons from High-Performing Hispanic Schools*. New York: Teachers College Press.

Roehrig, G. H., M. Dubosarsky, A. Mason, S. Carlson, and B. Murphy. 2011. "We Look More, Listen More, Notice More: Impact of Sustained Professional Development on Head Start Teachers' Inquiry-Based and Culturally-Relevant Science Teaching Practices." *Journal of Science Education and Technology* 20(5): 566–78.

Rogoff, B. 2003. *The Cultural Nature of Human Development*. Oxford, UK: Oxford University Press.

Santa Clara County Office of Education. 2016. "The My Name, My Identity Campaign." *My Name, My Identity.org*. www.mynamemyidentity.org.

Schubert, W. 2010. "Journeys of Expansion and Synopsis: Tensions in Books That Shaped Curriculum Inquiry, 1968–Present." *Curriculum Inquiry* 40(1): 17–94.

Scribner, S. 1970. "Which Agenda for Advocacy?" *Social Policy* 1: 40.

Sheets, R. H. 1995. "From Remedial to Gifted: Effects of Culturally Centered Pedagogy." *Theory into Practice* 34(3): 186–93.

Sleeter, C. 2012. "Confronting the Marginalization of Culturally Responsive Pedagogy." *Urban Education* 47: 562–84.

Souto-Manning, M. 2010a. *Freire, Teaching, and Learning: Culture Circles Across Contexts*. New York: Peter Lang.

———. 2010b. "Teaching English Learners: Building on Cultural and Linguistic Strengths." *English Education* 42(3): 249–63.

———. 2013. *Multicultural Teaching in the Early Childhood Classroom: Strategies, Tools, and Approaches, Preschool-2nd Grade*. Washington, DC: Association for Childhood Education International; New York: Teachers College Press.

Souto-Manning, M., and J. Martell. 2016. *Reading, Writing, and Talk: Inclusive Teaching Strategies for Diverse Learners, K–2*. New York: Teachers College Press.

Strauss, V. 2014. "Proposed Texas Textbooks Are Inaccurate, Biased and Politicized, New Report Finds." *The Washington Post*, September 12. www.washingtonpost.com/news/answer-sheet/wp/2014/09/12proposed-texas-textbooks-are-inaccurate-biased-and-politicized-new-report-finds.

Stuart, D., and D. Volk. 2002. "Collaboration in a Culturally Responsive Pedagogy: Educating Teachers and Latino Children." *Reading: Literacy and Language* 36: 127–34.

Suárez-Orozco, C., M. Suárez-Orozco, and I. Todorova. 2008. *Learning in a New Land: Immigrant Students in American Society*. Cambridge, MA: Harvard University Press.

Swadener, B. B., and S. Lubeck. 1995. *Children and Families "at Promise": Deconstructing the Discourse of Risk*. Albany, NY: State University of New York Press.

Tatum, B. D. 1997. *"Why Are All the Black Kids Sitting Together in the Cafeteria?" and Other Conversations About Race*. New York: Basic Books.

Tenery, M. F. 2005. "La visita." In *Funds of Knowledge: Theorizing Practices in Households, Communities, and Classrooms*, edited by N. González, L. C. Moll, and C. Amanti, 119–30. Mahwah, NJ: Lawrence Erlbaum Associates.

Texas Freedom Network. 2014. "Writing to the Standards: Reviews of Proposed Social Studies Textbooks for Texas Public Schools." http://tfn.org/cms/assets/uploads/2015/11/FINAL_executivesummary.pdf.

Tonatiuh, D. 2016. *The Princess and the Warrior: A Tale of Two Volcanoes*. New York: Abrams.

Valdés, G. 1996. *Con Respeto: Bridging the Distances Between Culturally Diverse Families and Schools*. New York: Teachers College Press.

Valenzuela, A. 1999. *Subtractive Schooling: U.S.-Mexican Youth and the Politics of Caring*. Albany, NY: State University of New York Press.

Villegas, A. M., and T. Lucas. 2002. *Educating Culturally Responsive Teachers: A Coherent Approach*. Albany, NY: State University of New York Press.

Yolen, J. 1992. *Encounter*. Illustrated by David Shannon. New York: Harcourt Brace Jovanovich.

Zinn, H. 2007/2009. *A Young People's History of the United States*. New York: Seven Stories Press.

———. 2015. *A People's History of the United States*. New York: HarperCollins.